From
Our Table
to Yours

From Our Table to Yours

A Collection of Filipino Heirloom Recipes & Family Memories

Angelo Comsti

Marshall Cavendish
Cuisine

Editor : Lydia Leong
Designer : Bernard Go Kwang Meng
Photographer : At Maculangan

Published by Marshall Cavendish Cuisine
An imprint of Marshall Cavendish International

Other Marshall Cavendish Offices:
Marshall Cavendish Corporation. 99 White Plains Road, Tarrytown NY 10591-9001, USA • Marshall
Cavendish International (Thailand) Co Ltd. 253 Asoke, 12th Flr, Sukhumvit 21 Road, Klongtoey
Nua, Wattana, Bangkok 10110, Thailand • Marshall Cavendish (Malaysia) Sdn Bhd, Times Subang,
Lot 46, Subang Hi-Tech Industrial Park, Batu Tiga, 40000 Shah Alam, Selangor Darul Ehsan, Malaysia

Marshall Cavendish is a trademark of Times Publishing Limited

National Library Board, Singapore Cataloguing-in-Publication Data

Comsti, Angelo, author.
From our table to yours : a collection of Filipino heirloom recipes & family memories /
Angelo Comsti. - Singapore : Marshall Cavendish Cuisine, [2013]
pages cm
ISBN : 978-981-4398-56-5 (paperback)

1. Cooking, Philippine. I. Title.

TX724.5.P5
641.59599 – dc23   OCN846533413

Printed in Singapore by KWF Printing Pte Ltd

ding habichue...
Iguisa qñg aceite, 2 binutil a...
...na, yabe la ning habichuelas a pepatic...
at paminta, isilbi la qñg bannejano maca pa...
...be itugtug ing salsa de tomates.

SALSA DE TOMATES:- 2 cuchara mantequilla o taba - 1...
...2 cuc... chara pure de tomtes - 1/2 tasa...
A LA ESPAÑOLA) chara pure de tomtes - 1/2...
buyas - 2 binutil a bauang sibuy...

...figuturan Qñg Mantequilla mapali ibili ing bauang si...
...harina yabe ing ditac a laman jamon a peñgili maimpis at...
...mapal... be na ing pure de tomates, caibat ing sabo o danum...

...y, ing
...nan di...

III

PASTEL DE LENGUA

...la ñila vaca - 2 chorizo - 4 a patatas - 1 a sib...
...balung laurel - 2 cuchara aslam - 1 a lata gui...
Ing ñila linisan ya, italbug ya qñg danum a...
...lu nang maputi. Calinis na titiang ya o ipalare...
...pamtian cuanan ing angang 5 cuchara ibili qñg...
...wiha, yabe ing 2 cuchara aslam ing sibuyas, bau...
...inan sabo o danum at ilutu na angang lambut ya...
Pañga lambut na ilaco ya qñg salsa at pañ...
...patatas at sanahorias a liga na at ing cho...
...caibat yabe ing ... iti qñg ditac a mantequilla,...
...capaliuas ning ... salsa ning ñila salacan at yabe o...
...ulian ing vainilla at clara at harina ..., tacpan lang paste, pulisand/il...
...pilisan mantequilla at harina ... harina (... tasa ... 100 grs...
...harita asin.

IV

...ernando, Pampanga
Junio 22, 1939

Dedication

My fascination for food started at home, where dishes are prepared with much care and thought, and meal times are made special by the company of every member of the family.

To the people responsible for feeding my hunger for food and life itself—my loving parents Eric and Cynthia, my siblings Carlo and Angela, Paul, Ria, and my nephews Pocholo and Joaquin, thank you for making every eating experience truly worthwhile, and more importantly, for allowing me to keep doing the things I love to do most: be a son, brother, uncle, friend and cook.

Here's to many more memorable feasts!

Angelo

Contents

Introduction

It started out of frustration, one that stemmed from a fervent longing to get my hands on a recipe for Filipino chiffon cake (*taisan*). It was by my grandmother's sister, and years after her passing and after many failed attempts, I still haven't come close to her version of the traditional chiffon slice. I miss eating it, but I know all is not lost as I still have memories of it to live by—like the aroma of the baked cake wafting throughout the house and hitting me upon entry or those times when I would catch Lola Ponying huddled over the countertop, brushing butter on the cake that just came hot off her white oven. You see, with my family, food always came with good memories and I realize that recalling these can be just as indulgent as enjoying a piece of that cake.

It was this that led me to put this book together, one that will not only store family recipes but also immortalize the personal stories that come with each of them. And I figured, with a cuisine as rich in history and flavours as ours, and one that is built on family feasts, it couldn't be any more fitting and practical. These recipes need to serve their purpose and they also need to be passed on, and what better way to do so than by preserving them in print.

As it is an endeavour that's close to me, I invited people in the industry whom I hold much respect for to join me in my advocacy. I was quite overwhelmed with how generous many of them were and even glad to find out that storing the recipes had been something some of them have long wanted to do, but never had the time to. Everything then fell into place and more than 50 recipes later, I found myself having a good and balanced mix of dishes—from easy-to-do fare such as fruit salad and a sandwich spread to slow food like tripe and chickpea stew (*callos*) and pork, chicken and beef in clear broth (*nilagang*); regional dishes like Cebu's ox tail and trotter stew (*balbacua*) and Pampanga's petito cookies to a family's take on a classic like the pineapple upside down cake.

Initially, it was only meant to be a recipe reference and an interesting biographical read. In the process though, it became even more personal with the inclusion of photos that have been dug from dusty albums. It is a great way to honour our parents, grandparents and whomever taught us how to cook. And it came out more wonderful than I ever imagined it to be. May this book become a delicious slice of local gastronomic history that will be preserved and feasted on by many.

"Food has become witness to many of our red-letter days. In fact, it has even become instrumental to how these moments have come to play. It gives comfort when we're downhearted, makes casual any business deal, lends courage when popping the question, and sparks conversations among families and drives them to lay everything out on the dining table. Such is its power and influence."

Contributors

Aileen Anastacio

With her delicious desserts, top-rating cooking shows, monthly magazine features, and bestselling cookbooks, Aileen is among the most recognized pastry chefs in the country. Her shop, Goodies N' Sweets, continues to provide such favourites as Turtle Pie, tiramisu, and her famous chocolate cake, Decadence.

Chona Ayson

Growing up with a mom who would tag her along in baking classes and make her birthday cakes year after year, Chona inevitably fell in love with baking, so much so that she opened Homemade Treasures, a made-to-order, home-based business in Porac, Pampanga, recognised for buttery *ensaymadas* and *sansrivals*.

  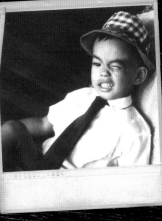 

Arnold Bernardo

Arnold used to help his hardworking mother with her side business, catering food for friends and clients. This fuelled his passion for food, leading him to enrol in culinary school, join cooking contests, winning one, and opening a business of his own— Deep Dips, a line of gourmet bottled goods.

Joel Binamira

Joel is a management consultant who has travelled and eaten his way around the world. He lets us in on all his culinary adventures via his website, marketmanila.com. Zubuchon, his restaurant, inspired by Anthony Bourdain's fondness for his roasted pig (*lechon*), recently opened its fourth branch in Cebu.

Joey de Larrazabal-Blanco

Miles away from home with nobody to feed her, Joey was forced to cook. And it did her good as she found herself loving it. Since then, she has experimented on many dishes, shares the recipes in her blog, 80 Breakfasts and in a local food magazine, and enjoys them with her whole family.

Gwen Jacinto-Cariño

Some of Gwen's loyal clients as an in-demand PR agent include a manufacturer of kitchen pans and an elusive restaurant group. She's no stranger when it comes to the food scene in Manila. In fact, she is a co-organiser of the successful Best Food Forward, a charity food fair, held annually.

Cynthia Comsti

With a mother and grandmother who loved playing in the kitchen and a bountiful backyard full of vegetables and fruits like jackfruit, mango, pomelo and even coffee beans, it wasn't hard for Cynthia to get busy cooking herself. Nowadays, she caters to small parties while successfully juggling responsibilities at home and in church.

Dedet dela Fuente

Former photographer and now, a doting single parent to three lovely girls, Dedet entered the local food scene with private degustation dinners under Pepita's Kitchen. She serves Filipino dishes that have been given her own unique spin. One of her bestsellers is her line of whole roasted pig (*lechon*) with different stuffings.

Jun Jun de Guzman

Jun Jun has long been a culinary instructor at the Center for Asian Culinary Studies (CACS) in the Philippines. Apart from being invited to cooking shows and being featured monthly in a local food magazine, he also keeps busy as a kitchen management consultant.

Antonio Escalante

The former flight attendant took professional culinary lessons in Adelaide, Australia before settling in Manila and opening shop in Tagaytay. His restaurant, Antonio's, has been in *The Mi1ele Guide's* list of the Top 20 Best Restaurants in Asia since its inception. He also owns and manages Antonio's Grill and Breakfast at Antonio's.

Maria Carmina Felipe

Back in the day when she was young and her siblings were already working, Carmina would prepare dinner for her family daily. She recalls, "The first thing I cooked was gelatin with cut-up bananas, placed in mugs. I was nine then." Today, she cooks for her own family, husband Leo and three boys.

Chin Gallegos

A former flight attendant, Chin has travelled the world and used that opportunity to hone her talent for cooking. Upon her return to Manila, she set up Pio's Kitchen, a private dining and catering company specialising in Spanish and Mediterranean cuisine. She is one of the few caterers who offers on-the-spot paella cooking.

Namee Jorolan

Namee always has her plate full. When she is in Pampanga, she helps out in her family's catering and restaurant business, the much-loved Everybody's Café. When she is in Manila, she fulfills food consultation responsibilities during the day and cooks thematic dinners under Pinoy Eats World at night.

Patricia Locsin

Patricia already knew what she wanted to be early in life. As a kid, she loved cooking spaghetti with meatballs for her dad. After finishing culinary studies, she interned at a hotel, worked at Cibo and Pepato restaurants, opened her own Good Earth restaurant, and has for five years now, worked as executive assistant and chef to Gaita Fores who has a string of successful restaurants.

Divine Enya Mesina

Divine has made a living out of her passion for food. Her foray into the industry began when she took on the role of a managing editor for a local food magazine. She has since opened a business selling fresh produce and gone into organic farming, which she has pledged to do for the rest of her life.

Camille Ocampo

At 20, Camille didn't know how to cook rice, but she loved eating desserts. Years later, she now has her own home-based business which is famous for her crème brûlée cake. She also teaches baking courses at ABS-CBN Foundation's Bayan Academy in the Philippines.

Myke Sarthou

Myke, or Chef Tatung to many, never thought he'd end up being a restaurateur. Cooking simply started out as a pastime, which led to hosting dinners for friends at home, and eventually to a city restaurant and a catering company. He has gained a loyal following and his clientele include celebrities and politicians.

Pixie Sevilla

Pixie is among the more recognisable names and faces in the local pastry industry. She has been on many shows and graced many publications. She has also won an international competition for her pastry. Her café, Forget Me Not Specialty Cakes, churns out goodies that always make it to many best desserts lists, including her recent line of products under Miel's Pastillerie.

Giney Villar

Giney used to work for a non-governmental organization, but now spearheads the operations at her own Adarna Food and Culture Restaurant, which allows people to enjoy things of the past—heirloom dishes and the old-world charm the place exudes.

Addie Wijangco

Juggling her duty as a hands-on mother to four young kids, Addie is also a home baker known for her soft and fluffy *ensaymadas*, made according to her grandmother's generations-old Kapampangan recipe. Many other shops and bakeries sell the same specialty, but hers is regarded as one of the best.

Vegetables & Noodles

Fried Pork Spring Rolls (Boquillos) 22

Heart of Palm Spring Roll (Lumpiang Ubod) 24

Parañaque Noodles (Pancit Parañaque) 26

Pork Macaroni Soup 28

Baked Beans with Bacon 30

Cynthia Comsti's

Fried Pork Spring Rolls (Boquillos)

shared by Angelo Comsti

Makes 50 pieces

My father's mother, Mama Bel, loved to cook. I can still recall the days when the whole family would troop over to her house in Sumilang, Pasig for Sunday lunch and I would see her cooking a cauldron of stew over burning wood. Mama Bel was used to cooking for large groups. In fact, every Holy Week, after the procession of religious statues, she would welcome neighbours and even strangers into her house for a meal. She was very giving and my mom is no different. She inherited this fried spring roll recipe from my grandmother and like her, she also displays generosity by cooking this and her other beloved dishes for the families of friends, her church group and neighbours.

cooking oil, as needed

3 cloves garlic, minced

500 g ground pork

$^1/_2$ cup dried shrimps (*hibi*), pounded

1 kg potatoes, peeled and chopped into small cubes

1 cup raisins

50 sheets fresh spring roll (*lumpia*) wrappers

4 hard-boiled eggs, peeled and cut into pieces

1. In a pan, heat oil and sauté garlic.

2. Add ground pork and stir-fry for 5 minutes.

3. Add ground dried shrimps and potatoes. Cook until potatoes are tender. Place in a bowl with raisins. Set aside to cool slightly.

4. When cool enough to handle, place 2 Tbsp pork mixture in a line across one corner of a spring roll wrapper. Top with some egg. Bring the corner of the wrapper over the filling, then roll tightly. Fold the right and left corners over and continue to roll tightly. Seal end with a brush of water. Repeat until ingredients are used up.

5. Heat oil for deep-frying and deep-fry spring rolls in batches until golden brown. Place on paper towels to drain excess oil. Serve.

Tasty Tip

For a condiment, combine 3 minced garlic cloves, 1 cup white vinegar and a teaspoon each of salt and sugar. Stir until dissolved. Add red bird's eye chili for a spicy kick!

"My mom always has a stack
of these hidden in the freezer for
times when she is too busy to cook."

Luisa Consing-Locsin's

Heart of Palm Spring Rolls
(Lumpiang Ubod)

shared by Patricia Locsin

Makes 20 pieces

From the time I was a kid up until now, my paternal grandmother, Lola Inday, would prepare this spring roll for Saturday lunch, family gatherings or whenever she's hosting an occasion. As this involves a lot of prep work, she had Manang Laida at her beck and call back in the day. Manang Laida was Lola Inday's cook for almost 30 years. But now, there's us, her grandchildren to help her do the cooking.

Lola has her unique way of preparing this dish. There was a time when I thought that her spring rolls were brown due to the heart of palm. But it wasn't so. It was due to the soy sauce and muscovado sugar, two ingredients not typical of a fresh spring roll. The addition of muscovado though does say a lot about the region of Negros, where my family hails from. It's not called The Land of Sugar for nothing.

¹/₄ cup vegetable oil

1 head garlic, peeled and minced

125 g shrimps, peeled, deveined and chopped

1 medium red onion, peeled and chopped

125 g ground pork

500 g heart of palm (*ubod*), chopped

3 Tbsp light soy sauce

¹/₃ cup muscovado sugar

20 sheets fresh spring roll (*lumpia*) wrappers

1. In a wok over medium to high heat, heat oil and sauté 1 tsp garlic until slightly coloured.

2. Add shrimps and onion and sauté for a minute. Add ground pork and continue to sauté. Add heart of palm and simmer in its rendered liquid for 10 minutes.

3. Add soy sauce and sugar. Cook, covered, for 10–15 minutes until liquid is reduced, but not totally dry. Remove from heat. Separate liquid from filling. Add remaining raw garlic to liquid. Mix well. Set liquid and filling aside to cool.

4. To assemble, spread ¹/₂ tsp raw garlic mix on a wrapper followed by 2 Tbsp filling. Bring edge of wrapper over filling and roll tightly. Fold left and right sides over filling and continue to roll up tightly. Seal end with a brush of water. Serve.

Tasty Tip

My family has always used Chan spring roll wrappers available from the Burgos Market in Bacolod. Mrs Lucy Chan is a third generation member of the family that has been making these thin, delicate wrappers for over 70 years now.

"These days, heart of palm
spring roll takes on a new form
as it is also served deep-fried."

Nana Ray's

Parañaque Noodles
(Pancit Parañaque)

shared by Dedet dela Fuente

Serves 6

Nana Ray was my grandfather's house help and she had much influence on the way I cook my favourite noodle dish. I grew up in Parañaque and beside my grandparents' house was the wet market, so it was very convenient to cook whatever we fancied. Sadly, Nana Ray passed away when I was just 15. But from the short time I knew her, I appreciated how wonderful a cook she was. And of the dishes she prepared, it is this and her *ginataan*, a dessert cooked with coconut milk, that really left an impression on me. She would cook it every time it was the city fiesta or there was a prayer meeting at our place. I honour her and the times we shared together by adapting her recipe to my food business and offering what I call the Birthday *Lechon*—a whole roasted pig stuffed with her Parañaque noodles.

250 g pig's cheeks, cut into 1-cm cubes

cooking oil, as needed

2 heads garlic, peeled and minced

1 medium white onion, peeled and chopped

salt and ground black pepper, to taste

3 cups water

5 Tbsp light soy sauce

200 g rice vermicelli (*pancit bihon*)

200 g thick egg noodles (*pancit miki*)

1 medium carrot, peeled and minced

$^1/_2$ head medium cabbage, chopped

2 stalks celery, minced

1 spring onion, chopped

1. Boil a pot of water and cook pig's cheeks until tender. Drain well.

2. In a pan, heat some oil and sauté garlic and onion until slightly coloured. Add pig's cheeks and sauté until browned. Season with salt and pepper.

3. Add water and soy sauce. Mix well and bring to a simmer.

4. Add vermicelli and cook for 3 minutes. Add egg noodles. Make sure there is enough liquid to simmer noodles.

5. Add carrot, cabbage, celery and spring onion. Simmer until noodles are cooked and vegetables are tender. Serve.

Tasty Tip
Serve with warm bread for a filling meal.

"We had a pigpen and Nana Ray used to take care of our two beloved piglets, Pork and Beans."

Urbana Victorino's

Pork Macaroni Soup

shared by Cynthia Comsti

Serves 4 to 6

There was a time when Rizal High School used to be the only high school in the whole of Rizal. And since Lelang Banang, my maternal grandmother, lived right across from the school, the businesswoman in her decided to set up a boarding house as well as a canteen to cater to the students. Her eatery did not only haul in students though. It drew in politicians as well! Her food was just that good. This soup was served in the canteen and at our home as an everyday dish. Nowadays, mom has it prepared by her cook once in a blue moon. I've never cooked this for my family because I'm quite sure they won't like it. I, however, still do.

cooking oil, as needed

3 cloves garlic, peeled and minced

2 medium white onions, peeled and chopped

500 g chicken liver

1 kg pig brains, cut into chunks

6 cups rice wash

1 cup uncooked macaroni

1 Tbsp fish sauce

2.5-cm knob ginger, peeled and cut into thin strips

1. In a pot, heat some oil and sauté garlic and onions until onions are translucent.
2. Add chicken liver and pig brains and continue to sauté.
3. Add rice wash and bring to the boil.
4. Add macaroni, fish sauce and ginger. Lower heat and simmer until macaroni is tender. Serve.

Tasty Tip

The rice wash is obtained by washing 2–3 cups raw rice in 6 cups water. It can be substituted with plain water.

"I miss having this especially since I have not come across it in any restaurant in Manila."

Maruja Lopez-Veloso's

Baked Beans with Bacon

shared by Patricia Locsin

Serves 4

My grandmother Lola Ua and I once made a deal. I had to do something for her before I could indulge in her dishes. It was either I helped her set the table, then wash the dirty pots and pans after, or for us to converse in Spanish. Since her food was simply too good to resist, I easily gave in to the bribe. Hence, I ballooned to 63.5 kg back in elementary school! For this dish alone, I didn't think twice of fulfilling her request. For many of us, bacon is heaven. Serve it with plain rice and we're all good. But served with my Ua's baked beans, it's nothing less than the best.

6 slices bacon

¹/₄ cup olive oil

1 medium white onion, peeled and diced

1 piece Chorizo de Bilbao, chopped

2 420-g cans baked beans

¹/₄ cup yellow mustard

³/₄ cup tomato ketchup

1 cup packed brown sugar

1. Preheat oven to 180°C (350°F).

2. In a pan over medium heat, cook bacon to render some of the fat. Remove bacon and place on paper towels to drain excess oil.

3. In the same pan, heat olive oil and sauté onion until caramelised.

4. Add chorizo, baked beans, mustard, ketchup and sugar. Stir until sugar is dissolved. Transfer to a baking dish and top with bacon strips.

5. Bake uncovered for 30–40 minutes, or until bacon is crispy. Serve.

"Serve with a piece of baguette
as it makes for the perfect vessel
to mop up all the lovely sauce with."

Poultry

Chicken Stew with Fish Sauce
(Talunang Manok) 34

Tropical Chicken Casserole 36

Pineapple Chicken
(Pininyahang Manok) 38

Chicken Liver Adobo 40

Chicken Fricassee 42

Chicken Asado (Asado de Carajay) 44

Garlic Chicken 46

Chicken Stew (Chicken Estofado) 48

Dioscora de Guzman's

Chicken Stew with Fish Sauce
(Talunang Manok)

shared by Jun Jun de Guzman

Serves 4 to 6

We are four siblings—all boys and all of us can cook, when needed. In our family, the aroma of food that's being cooked easily lures us into the kitchen. However, our mom would usually drive us away, thinking we would only be bothersome to her process. Of the four, it was my youngest brother, Enrique, and I who managed to formulate our mom's recipes. She never gave us the exact measurements and so we both had to test and come up with them ourselves.

The meat in this dish can be tough that's why it is braised for quite a while. You might be taken aback the first time you try it as the saltiness of the fish sauce, the sourness of the vinegar and the biting flavour of ginger produce a strong and overwhelming taste. It is an acquired taste, which all four of us siblings fortunately have.

¹/₂ cup corn oil

2 Tbsp minced garlic

4 medium white onions, peeled and sliced

1 kg chicken, cut into serving pieces

3 Tbsp white vinegar

2 Tbsp finely chopped ginger

2 Tbsp light soy sauce

1 cup water

1 Tbsp fish sauce

freshly ground black pepper, to season

1. In a pan, heat oil and sauté garlic and onions until onions are translucent. Add chicken and cook until fat is rendered.

2. Add vinegar and ginger. Let boil for 3–5 minutes, without stirring, until sour aroma is gone. Mix.

3. Add soy sauce and water. Simmer for 2 minutes.

4. Add fish sauce and pepper. Simmer for a minute. Serve.

Tasty Tip

You can replace chicken with short ribs to come up with another Navotas favourite—*pinatisang* ribs.

"This dish is named talunang manok (literally defeated chicken) because it was traditionally made using the rooster that loses in a cockfight."

Amanda Makabali's

Tropical Chicken Casserole

shared by Chin Gallegos

Serves 10 to 15

My grandmother loved to entertain. She would cook a number of dishes, don a dress, do up her coiffed hair and lay out her antique china. And so it's no mystery why my cousins often headed out to Pampanga where my grandmother stayed, knowing the trip would guarantee great meals and memorable dining experiences. When she moved to our house in Quezon City after the Mount Pinatubo eruption, my relatives followed. Our house soon became sort of a transit house. Some even stayed for long periods of time! Even then, my grandmother never lost her role as the perfect hostess. During Christmas, she would typically be holed up in the kitchen preparing a whole array of dishes, including this delectable chicken dish.

1 kg potatoes, peeled and cut into cubes

60 g butter, plus more for topping

1 cup milk

salt and ground black pepper, to season

1 kg whole chicken, cut into pieces

cooking oil, as needed

3 white onions, peeled and chopped

1 head garlic, peeled and minced

1 400-g can button mushrooms, drained and sliced

1 290-g can cream of mushroom soup

$^1/_2$ cup cream

1 420-g can corn kernels, drained

chopped parsley, to garnish

1. In a pot with water, boil potatoes. Once soft, drain water and transfer potatoes to a bowl. Add butter and milk. Mash and mix until well incorporated. Season with salt and pepper. Set aside.

2. In a fresh pot of water, boil chicken just until cooked. Remove chicken and set aside to cool. Reserve liquid. When cool enough to handle, pick meat off chicken bones and shred. Set aside.

3. In a deep pan, heat some oil and sauté onions, garlic and mushrooms until onions are translucent. Add shredded chicken and mix well.

4. Pour in cream of mushroom soup, cream and 1 cup reserved liquid. Season with salt and pepper. Let simmer until mixture is creamy.

5. Preheat oven to 180°C (350°F).

6. Transfer chicken mixture to a casserole dish. Top with a layer of mashed potatoes and spread evenly. Scatter corn kernels over and dot with some butter.

7. Bake for 30 minutes or until top is golden brown. Garnish with chopped parsley.

"This casserole is akin to a pot pie and to date, I have no clue why my grandmother called this dish tropical."

Cynthia Comsti's

Pineapple Chicken
(Pininyahang Manok)

shared by Angelo Comsti

Serves 4

It was just a couple of years back when I developed a fixation for anything sweet and salty. And it wasn't just with the desserts—I went crazy with all the salted caramel pastries that hit the town last year! I also share the same sentiment with savoury dishes, that's why I undeniably love my mom's pineapple chicken (*pininyahang manok*). The sweetness of the ripe pineapple chunks matched with salty sauce—it makes my mouth water just thinking about it. My mom would stir in condensed milk just before serving the dish and I remember despising it the first time, thinking it was a chicken dessert. But once I had a mouthful, I was taken by surprise and have since then been addicted.

500 g chicken breast fillet, cut into bite-size pieces

salt and ground black pepper, to season

cooking oil, as needed

4 cloves garlic, peeled and minced

1 large white onion, peeled and chopped

1 Tbsp fish sauce

1 420-g can pineapple chunks, drained

³/₄ cup water

3 Tbsp condensed milk

sugar, to taste

chopped spring onions, to garnish

1. Season chicken with salt and pepper.

2. In a deep pan, heat oil and sauté garlic and onion until onion is translucent.

3. Add chicken and sauté until lightly coloured.

4. Add fish sauce and pineapple chunks and sauté for a minute.

5. Pour in water and condensed milk. Stir and simmer for a minute.

6. Sprinkle with sugar and mix until sugar is dissolved. Transfer to a serving dish. Garnish with spring onions. Serve.

Tasty Tip

Condensed milk, not sweetened condensed milk is used in this recipe. If using sweetened condensed milk, simply omit the addition of sugar and adjust the sweetness of the dish according to your preference.

"When eating this, make sure that each mouthful is made up of a piece of chicken, a chunk of pineapple and a spoonful of rice that has already been doused with the sauce. Everything just goes so well together."

Evelyn Morato Ocampo's

Chicken Liver Adobo

shared by Camille Ocampo

Serves 4 to 6

This recipe hails from my grandmother's province. She was born in the municipality of Casiguran in Quezon, where many of my favourite food products like coconut jam and *paho*, a breed of small mangoes, also come from. My grandmother didn't cook many dishes, but of the few that she did, she did them very well. This dish was my mom's favourite growing up. My mother, Evelyn, with the help of my late grandmother's cook, always prepared this dish for our trips to the beach or Tagaytay when we were younger.

500 g chicken, cut into serving pieces

$^1/_2$ Tbsp whole black peppercorns

$1^1/_2$ cups white vinegar

500 g chicken liver

$^1/_2$ cup water

1 bay leaf

1 chicken stock cube

salt and ground black pepper, to taste

1. Place chicken, peppercorns and vinegar in a medium pot. Bring to the boil, then lower heat and simmer for 7 minutes.

2. Add chicken liver and cook until tender. Remove liver and purée with water in a blender. Return purée to the pot along with bay leaf and chicken stock cube. Season with salt and pepper.

3. Continue to simmer until sauce is thick and slightly dry. Serve.

Tasty Tip
Adobo keeps well and always tastes better when served the following day, reheated, and with the meat falling off the bones.

"This dish has become part of my heritage and I've grown to love adobo that's not cooked in soy sauce."

Antonia del Valle Ortega's

Chicken Fricassee

shared by Gwen Jacinto-Cariño

Serves 4 to 6

My maternal grandmother not only likes to cook, but she also likes to make her own version of traditional dishes—even her own family's heirloom recipes saw a little experimentation. This particular dish came about when she wanted to put a new spin on plain old fried chicken. She thought of adding sauce to make it more exciting. Consequently, it resulted in a creamy and tasty chicken dish, which my mom inherited and first cooked for me when I was six years old.

1 whole chicken, cut into serving pieces

salt and ground black pepper, to season

1 cup plain (all-purpose) flour

cooking oil, as needed

3/4 cup water

1/4 cup evaporated milk

1 tsp cornflour (cornstarch), mixed with 1 tsp water

12 green beans, trimmed and cut in half crosswise

1. Season chicken with salt and pepper, then dredge in flour until fully coated.

2. In a deep pan, heat oil and deep-fry chicken until light brown and slightly crisp. Remove and place on paper towels to drain excess oil.

3. In another deep pan, place chicken and pour in water. Bring to the boil.

4. When water is boiling, lower heat to a simmer. Add evaporated milk and cornflour slurry. Stir gently and simmer until chicken is fully cooked.

5. Add green beans and cook until tender. Season with salt and pepper to taste. Serve.

"Growing up, I preferred this over fried chicken because I liked my food with some sauce. To this day, I still am not a big fan of dry food."

Medy Enriquez Rodrigo's

Chicken Asado (Asado de Carajay)

shared by Pixie Sevilla

Serves 6

Everybody who came by our house for Sunday lunch and was served this dish would usually request for the recipe. To me, that was quite a mystery because I grew up having it often and didn't see what the fuss was about. In fact, I remember not liking it so much the first time I made it. For a kilo or a kilo and a half of chicken, we used nine large onions! I was a teenager when I was asked to prepare it and I remember smelling bad after. Also, I cried buckets after slicing all those onions! It was hard to make because when I did it, I was still young. But now that I am much older, it doesn't seem so complicated to do after all. I guess it was just too much for me to make at such an early age. Now when I make it, my daughter Miel indulges on the sauce and eats it alone with rice. She hates onions, but doesn't know just how much of it is incorporated in the dish!

1 cup light soy sauce

juice from 10 calamansi limes

1.5 kg chicken, cut into serving pieces

cooking oil, as needed

1 head garlic, peeled and minced

9 medium white onions, peeled and finely chopped

1 cup water

1. In a big bowl, combine soy sauce and calamansi juice. Add chicken, cover and leave to marinate in the refrigerator overnight.

2. Remove chicken from marinade and reserve marinade.

3. In a deep pan, heat oil and half-cook chicken by frying the pieces just until golden brown. Place on paper towels to drain excess oil.

4. In another pan, heat some oil and sauté garlic and onions until onions are translucent. Add reserved marinade and water. Bring to the boil.

5. Add chicken and lower heat. Simmer until chicken is cooked all the way through. Serve.

"The local name for this chicken dish comes from the carajay, a cooking pan shaped like a wok, typically used to cook this dish."

Antonia del Valle Ortega's

Garlic Chicken

shared by Gwen Jacinto-Cariño

Serves 4 to 6

My mother's family, the Ortegas, love cooking, but none of them went to a formal culinary school except for my aunt Helen, and yet the kids, all eight of them, found pleasure in helping out in the kitchen. Mama Toni, as we fondly call our grandmother, had written down her recipes by hand and kept them. This allowed her siblings to have their own copies of her dishes. This included my mom, Nonette, who had hers written on index cards and placed in an old wooden box. I'm fortunate to have been its recipient when she migrated to the US.

Of all the recipes in the box, this is the one I find myself cooking a lot of, firstly, because it can be done in less than 30 minutes, and also because it has been proven, time and again, to be a hit. Mama Toni, as I recall, cooked it without the mushrooms. That idea came from my mom.

4 Tbsp unsalted butter, softened

2 Tbsp canola oil

1 head garlic, peeled and crushed

1 whole chicken, cut into serving pieces

1 284-g can button mushrooms, sliced, liquid in can reserved

$^1/_4$ cup evaporated milk

salt and ground black pepper, to season

1. In a large pan, heat butter and oil. Add garlic and sauté until slightly golden.

2. Season chicken with salt and pepper. Add to pan and fry until golden brown.

3. Add mushrooms and sauté lightly.

4. Add evaporated milk and 3 Tbsp liquid from can of mushrooms. Simmer until chicken is fully cooked. Adjust seasoning to taste. Serve.

"My father would always ask my mom to cook this for him and she would happily do so."

Mary Angara Morato's

Chicken Stew (Chicken Estofado)

shared by Camille Ocampo

Serves 4 to 6

On our dining table, there always had to be a chicken dish served along with the bean stew (*fabada*). Oftentimes, it was rotisserie chicken. Other times, it was this. There was a stage when we frequently had roast pork and steaks. And then I witnessed the change in eating habits when we eventually got served more white meat and dishes cooked in olive oil.

This is one of those dishes even kids love to eat—in our family, at least. As opposed to the other dishes that my grandmother used to prepare, this is the one dish that many have attempted to copy. It's everyone's secret go-to recipe because it's accessible yet not that common. It's simple in theory and so my mom, my sisters and I have all tried to make it. Still, my grandmother makes the best version.

1 whole chicken, cut into serving pieces

salt and ground black pepper, to season

2 heads garlic, left unpeeled; separated into cloves

3 medium white onions, peeled and chopped

olive oil, as needed

half a chicken stock cube

3 Tbsp liquid seasoning

1 Tbsp dark rum

$1/4$ cup green olives, pitted and chopped

1 155-g can mushrooms, drained and sliced

1. Season chicken with salt and pepper. Lay the pieces flat in a wok or a large pan. Scatter garlic and onions around. Pour in enough olive oil to cover all the ingredients.

2. Place over low heat and cook until chicken is soft and tender, and cooked all the way through.

3. Add chicken stock cube, liquid seasoning and dark rum. Stir.

4. Add olives and mushrooms and cook just until heated through. Serve.

"My family's chicken stew does not look sophisticated. In fact, it's a mess of a dish, swimming in oil when cooking."

Meat

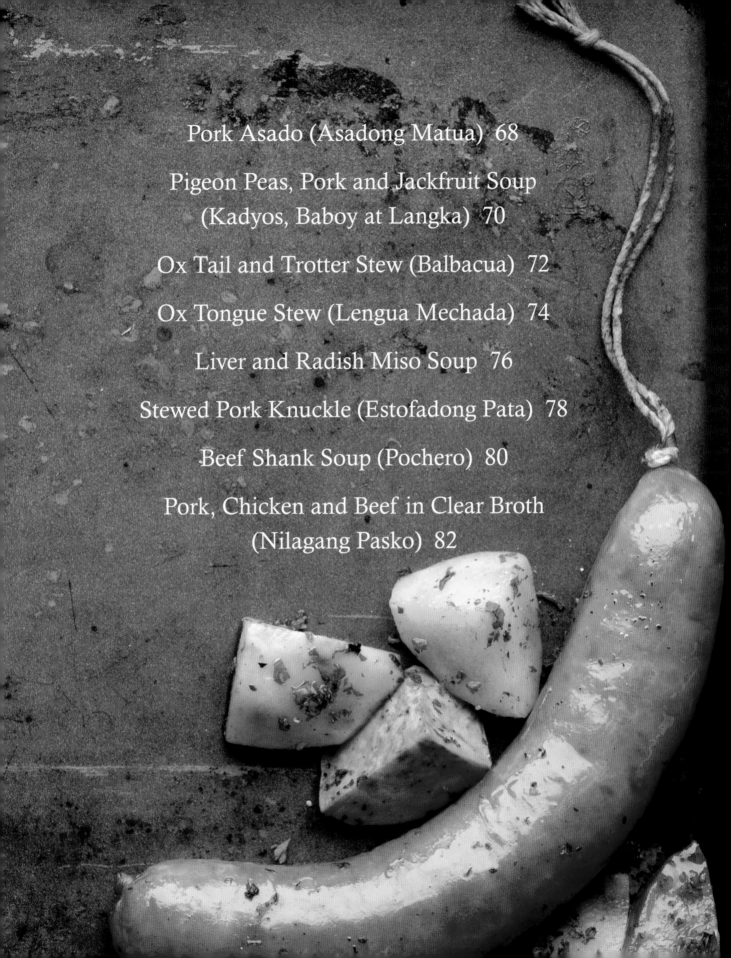

Gloria Rodriguez Guanzon's

Creamy Luncheon Meat Spread

shared by Addie Wijangco

Serves 4 to 6

There are many dishes that remind me of my grandmother, but of the lot, this is the one that feels closest to home. This is something my grandmother used to make often, especially when we had family trips. It's our official *baon* (stock of food). And she made it in bulk so that we would always have something to munch on during long road trips. For something that's so simple and easy-to-do, this sandwich spread brings me comfort.

2¼ cups evaporated milk

2 Tbsp butter

2 Tbsp plain (all-purpose) flour

3 cups minced luncheon meat

salt, to taste

ground nutmeg, to taste

1. In a pan, warm evaporated milk over low to medium heat.

2. In a separate pan, melt butter.

3. Add flour to melted butter and mix with a wooden spoon until there are no visible lumps.

4. Add warm milk gradually, stirring continuously until creamy.

5. Add luncheon meat, salt and nutmeg to taste. Mix well.

6. Remove from heat and leave to cool. Spread generously on bread and serve.

"It's true when they say, that the simplest of things are often the best ones."

Angelita Virrey Bernardo's

Corned Beef

shared by Arnold Bernardo

Serves 4 to 6

I don't know if it was a good thing or a bad thing, but when I tried this for the first time, I knew I could never go back to eating canned corned beef ever again! Whatever brand you serve me, I'm quite sure it won't compare to how delicious my mom's corned beef is. That's why, I always have it in stock in my freezer. And whenever the craving arises, I just thaw, sauté and have it for breakfast along with fried rice, an egg cooked sunny side up and caramelised onions. The beef is cubed, not shredded and does not come in a slab either. I also tweaked my mom's recipe by adding a few key ingredients to enhance the flavour. It's so simple and yet so good.

7 cloves garlic, peeled and crushed

1 small white onion, peeled and chopped

2 Tbsp salt

2 Tbsp brown sugar

4 cups water

1 kg beef brisket, trimmed and cut into cubes

1 large red onion, peeled and quartered

$1/4$ tsp ground cayenne pepper

1. Place 3 cloves garlic, white onion, salt, sugar and 1 cup water in a bowl. Stir until salt and sugar are dissolved.

2. Add beef, cover and allow to marinate in the refrigerator for at least 10 hours.

3. Drain marinated beef cubes and place in a deep pot.

4. Pour in 3 cups water and add red onion, 4 cloves garlic and cayenne pepper. Place over medium to high heat and bring to the boil.

5. When mixture is boiling, lower heat and simmer for about 30 minutes or until beef is tender. Skim off any impurities that accumulate on the surface from time to time. Remove beef from broth and serve.

Tasty Tip

To prolong the shelf life of this dish, add 1 tsp Prague powder (a tinted curing mixture also known as pink salt) when dissolving the salt and sugar for marinating the beef.

"I can never go back to eating canned corned beef after having something this good!"

Purificacion Abueva Binamira's

Roast Pig Congee (Lechon Pospas)

shared by Joel Binamira

Serves 4 to 6

This calming, restorative dish was almost always cooked when we were sick or out of sorts. My mom's version was a classic chicken congee that was relatively bland, though redolent of ginger, and served at the height of illness. This roast pig congee is a result of my recent pre-occupation with all things to do with roasted pig (*lechon*), and its flavour comes from the tasty and decadent broth. The broth and toppings are what take the basic congee to the next level!

2 Tbsp lard

5-cm knob ginger, peeled and sliced thinly lengthwise

1 white onion, peeled and chopped

3 cloves garlic, peeled and minced

3 cups water

1¹/₂ cups uncooked rice

a pinch of safflower or saffron

chopped deep-fried pork rind

chopped spring onions

minced fried garlic

calamansi juice, to taste

fish sauce, to taste

Broth

leftover roast pig bones

water, as needed

1 white onion, peeled and chopped

a handful of spring onions

1 bay leaf

a handful of celery leaves

Roasted Pig Flakes

leftover roasted pig

light soy sauce, to taste

calamansi juice, to taste

ground black pepper, to taste

2 Tbsp lard

1. To make broth, place bones in a stockpot and cover with water. Add onion, spring onions, bay leaf and celery leaves. Simmer over low heat for 2–3 hours. Strain and cool. Measure out 3 cups broth for use in congee. Any leftover broth can be stored in the freezer.

2. To prepare roasted pig flakes, shred leftover meaty pieces of roasted pig by hand (or with two forks) into roughly 5-cm long pieces. Drizzle with soy sauce and calamansi juice. Season with freshly ground black pepper. Melt lard in a pan and fry roasted pig shreds until lightly golden brown and crispy. Set aside.

3. In a large pot over medium heat, melt lard. Add ginger and sauté for a minute or until fragrant. Add onion and garlic and sauté for another minute or until fragrant and onion is translucent.

4. Add broth and water. Bring to a simmer. Add rice and stir to prevent rice from sticking to the bottom of the pot. Bring to a low simmer, stirring every once in a while, paying closer attention to the pot after 10 minutes of cooking.

5. Add safflower or saffron for a tinge of colour and flavour. When rice is fully cooked, turn off heat and serve hot. Do not allow to sit as the rice may absorb all of the liquid and turn quite thick.

6. Serve congee with roasted pig flakes, pork rind, spring onions and fried garlic. Adjust to taste with calamansi juice and fish sauce.

Tasty Tip

When reheating leftover congee, add a little water or broth to thin the consistency.

"Pospas was the Visayan term used
in our home to describe arroz caldo,
congee or rice porridge."

Consolacion Fuentes's

Beef Stew (Beef Caldereta)

shared by Angelo Comsti

Serves 6 to 10

My mom's love for cooking is deeply rooted in her family's treasure trove of good eats as well as her mother's flair for preparing them. Known to us as Lola Nene, my maternal grandmother has become synonymous with her much-loved beef stew (*caldereta*). It's the one dish I fondly remember her by. And although my grandmother no longer has the capability to cook, my mom is the one who appeases our *caldereta* craving occasionally. I would simply pour the rich sauce on the rice and that would already make me a very happy camper. Sometimes, I'd sneak into the kitchen and without telling my mom, steal the stew left over from the day before and enjoy it at my own place.

$^1/_4$ cup butter, unsalted

1 kg beef cubes, cut into serving pieces

1 clove garlic, peeled and crushed

1 medium white onion, peeled and thinly sliced

10 whole black peppercorns

1 tsp white sugar

2 Tbsp light soy sauce

3 Tbsp Worcestershire sauce

$^1/_2$ cup tomato sauce

2 cups hot water

3 medium capsicums (bell peppers) of various colours, deseeded and diced

2 medium potatoes, peeled and chopped into medium cubes

1 large carrot, peeled and chopped into medium cubes

$^1/_2$ cup liver spread

$^1/_2$ cup grated Cheddar cheese

a dash of hot sauce

1. In a pot, melt butter and sear beef cubes until browned. Add garlic and onion. Sauté until onion is translucent.

2. Add peppercorns, sugar, soy sauce, Worcestershire sauce and tomato sauce. Mix for a minute, then add hot water. Cover and simmer until beef is close to tender.

3. Add capsicums, potatoes, carrot and liver spread. Continue to simmer until beef is tender and vegetables are cooked all the way through.

4. Add grated cheese and hot sauce. Mix. Serve.

Tasty Tip
If desired, you can mix in 1 cup of pitted olives just before serving.

"This stew has satisfied generations of appetites—from my lola's family and our family, and now to my nephew Pocholo Miguel who would help himself to three servings of caldereta each time it is served!"

Tomas Morato's

Bean Stew (Fabada)

shared by Camille Ocampo

Serves 4 to 6

My great grandfather was an immigrant from Spain who went on to become the first mayor of Quezon City. On his voyage here, he brought with him recipes from his homeland. Generations have passed and now all of his children's families have their own recipe for bean stew (*fabada*)—a tweaked and personalised version of the original. It's funny because given the different versions, we didn't turn the situation into a *fabada*-off, a competition of sorts, but more of a mutual affection towards each other's dishes. I grew up loving the version my grandmother, Mary Angara Morato, used to cook. It has been served every single Sunday for lunch and family members react violently when it is a no-show on the table.

1 cup white beans

1 head garlic, peeled

1 medium yellow onion, peeled and chopped

1 ham bone

1 125-g pork leg

9 cups water

7 slices bacon, chopped

200 g Spanish chorizo, cut into bite-size pieces

1 1/2 cups tomato sauce

salt and ground black pepper, to taste

1. Soak beans in water overnight. The water level should be at least 8-cm above the beans. Drain.

2. In a large pot, boil beans, garlic, onion, ham bone and pork leg in water for 1 hour or until beans are almost tender. Remove ham bone and pork leg and leave to cool slightly. When cool enough to handle, remove meat from pork leg and cut into bite-size pieces.

3. In a frying pan, render fat from bacon and chorizo. Add pork leg meat and sauté for 5 minutes. Add tomato sauce and season with salt and pepper to taste.

4. Return meat mixture to pot. Simmer for about 25 minutes until stew is thick. Serve warm.

Tasty Tip

This is best paired with crusty bread, which can be used to mop up the flavourful sauce off the bowl.

"We always make a big pot of this bean stew, so the leftovers can show up mid-week."

Amanda Makabali's

Tripe and Chickpea Stew (Callos)

shared by Chin Gallegos

Serves 10 to 15

Many homes and buildings in San Fernando, Pampanga were greatly damaged when Mount Pinatubo erupted in 1991. The second floor of the Makabali Hospital became the first floor as the whole ground level got covered with mudflow. My grandmother's house suffered the same fate and she had to move in with us in Quezon City. I was 16 then and my taste buds got exposed to a whole new world as she cooked for the family every day. Among my siblings, I was the only one who was really interested in cooking, and I would hang out in the kitchen and watch how things were done. That's when I witnessed how this tripe and chickpea stew was made—from scratch.

500 g beef leg, cut into 2.5-cm thick slices

500 g tripe

500 g sirloin beef, cut into cubes

5 cloves garlic, peeled and minced

2 medium white onions, peeled and chopped

2 bay leaves

3 whole black peppercorns

6 cups water

1¹/₂ Tbsp olive oil

1 medium carrot, peeled and cut into cubes

1 medium red capsicum (bell pepper), deseeded and diced

1 210-g can Chorizo de Bilbao, sliced

1 150-g can chickpeas (garbanzos), drained

1 Tbsp smoked paprika

salt and ground black pepper, to season

1 400-g can whole peeled tomatoes

3 Tbsp grated Cheddar cheese

1. Boil beef leg, tripe and sirloin beef cubes separately, 2–3 times. Drain and place in a pot with 3 garlic cloves, 1 onion, bay leaves, black peppercorns and water. Simmer over low heat for 4–6 hours or until meat is tender and meat from beef leg falls off the bone. Set aside to cool.

2. Chop meat from beef leg and tripe into pieces. Set aside all meat. Reserve broth.

3. In a deep pan, heat olive oil and sauté remaining garlic and onion, carrot, capsicum, chorizo and chickpeas. Season with smoked paprika, salt and pepper.

4. Add meat and about 2 cups of broth. Simmer for 10 minutes.

5. Add tomatoes and simmer for another 15–20 minutes.

6. Remove from heat. Add cheese and allow it to melt into the stew. Serve.

Tasty Tip

To shorten your cooking time, you may use a pressure cooker.

"My grandmother would cook this dish even when she got too old to remember the ingredients. Once, she almost added cream instead of cheese!"

Manuel Villasin Escalante's

Gingered Pork and Liver Soup (Bas-Oy)

shared by Antonio Escalante

Serves 8 to 10

Many families in Bacolod have their own version of this dish. I know one family that cooks it with ground pork, while we prepare it using pork tenderloin that has been cut into strips and liver that has been grilled. It's done in different ways, but everyone in Bacolod knows about this dish—or at least, some form of it. It's similar to *batchoy*, a noodle soup made with pork organs, and we usually have it for brunch or as an afternoon snack. The recipe came from my paternal grandfather, Manuel, but I learned it from one of his cooks, Topacio, whom I watched intently whenever he cooked it for the family.

1 kg whole pork liver

2 Tbsp canola oil

1 large white onion, peeled and finely chopped

1 head garlic, peeled and roughly chopped

4-cm knob ginger, peeled and cut into thin strips

1 kg pork tenderloin, cut into thin strips

2 bundles lemon grass, ends trimmed and bruised

8 cups water

10 spring onions, chopped

salt and ground black pepper, to taste

1. Grill liver over charcoal until both sides are done. Cut into strips and set aside.

2. In a pot, heat oil and sauté onion until caramelised. Add garlic and ginger. Sauté for a minute.

3. Add pork tenderloin and grilled liver. Cook until pork turns light brown.

4. Add lemon grass and water. Bring to the boil, then lower heat and simmer for 20 minutes.

5. Remove lemon grass. Add spring onions. Season with salt and pepper to taste. Serve.

Tasty Tip

Grilling the pork liver over charcoal will add flavour and colour to the soup. The same goes with the onions. When caramelised, the onions will colour the soup and deliver a sweet flavour.

"We usually eat this dish with pandesal (Filipino bread roll) and not with rice."

Leonila Felipe's

Stuffed Pork Braised in Pineapple Juice (Hamonado)

shared by Maria Carmina Felipe

Serves 4 to 6

My mother-in-law got this recipe from her neighbour. During her childhood, there were no caterers, just people who would cook for big groups of people, and her neighbour would often receive requests to cook for weddings. During such functions, the guests would usually be raving about her food. True enough, when my mother-in-law got to taste her version of this dish, she liked it so much that she just had to learn how to prepare it herself. First, she watched her neighbour at work, then eventually, she mustered up the guts to ask for the recipe. She put her own twist to it and personalised the dish with the addition of a few more ingredients.

1 kg pork cutlet, thinly sliced

1 Tbsp iodised salt

6 Tbsp white sugar

2 cups unsweetened pineapple juice

4 Tbsp margarine, softened

1 439-g can crushed pineapple

90 g Cheddar cheese, cut into sticks

a handful of coriander leaves

3 hot dogs

cooking oil, as needed

1¹/₂ cups plain (all-purpose) flour

1. Rub pork with salt and sugar. Place in a deep dish and pour in enough pineapple juice just to cover meat. Cover and leave to marinate in the refrigerator overnight.

2. Remove pork from marinade. Reserve marinade.

3. Place pork on a flat work surface. Spread with margarine, then top with a layer of crushed pineapple, followed by cheese and coriander leaves. Arrange hot dogs in a row along the length of pork cutlet. Roll pork up tightly and tie with kitchen twine. Slice into half if pork roll is too big to handle.

4. Heat oil in a deep pan. Coat pork roll with flour, then gently lower into hot oil and fry until light brown.

5. In another deep pan, heat remaining pineapple juice and reserved marinade over low to medium heat. Add fried pork roll and cook for 15–20 minutes until meat is tender. Remove pork roll and set aside to cool. Continue to simmer pineapple juice until liquid is reduced to the consistency of syrup.

6. Slice pork and serve with sauce.

Tasty Tip
You can have your butcher slice the pork thinly and ready for rolling.

"I would always request my mother-in-law to cook this for Christmas Eve. Amazingly, it would taste the same every time—just perfect!"

Apung Mameng's

Pork Asado (Asadong Matua)

shared by Namee Jorolan

Serves 6

Pork asado (*asadong matua* or *asadong barrio* as it is also called), takes the place of ham or roast pork at our table on Christmas Eve. It's carved at the table and has become a holiday staple at my grandparents' house. Most of the dishes served on Christmas are often prepared in advance, as early as December 23, as they taste better with keeping.

When I was younger, I used to wonder why there were red thorns in this dish. They turned out to be pieces of tomato peel that just curled up upon cooking. You see, back in the day, we didn't skin our tomatoes. And that's a telltale sign that fresh tomatoes were used and not the canned ones. It's better to use native tomatoes for they have a more concentrated flavour, are juicier and aren't as watery as imported tomatoes.

cooking oil, as needed

1 kg pork shoulder

2 medium onions, peeled and sliced

1 clove garlic, peeled and minced

250 g tomatoes, sliced

5 Tbsp light soy sauce

$^1/_2$ cup tomato sauce

4 cups water

$^1/_2$ cup freshly-squeezed calamansi juice

salt and ground black pepper, to taste

1. In a pan, heat some oil and sear pork on all sides. If using a small pan, slice pork into smaller pieces to sear. Remove seared meat and discard excess oil. Set aside.

2. In the same pan, sauté onions, garlic and tomatoes over medium heat. Cook until tomatoes are soft. Add soy sauce and tomato sauce. Mix well.

3. Return meat to pan and cook for a few minutes in sauce. Add water and bring to the boil.

4. When water is boiling, lower heat to a simmer. Add calamansi juice. Cover and cook until liquid is almost evaporated and meat is tender.

5. Season with salt and pepper to taste. Slice and serve.

Tasty Tip
This dish is typically eaten with boiled potatoes.

"Our family used to cook many dishes, including this one, days before Christmas so there would be enough food to last us until the New Year."

Manuel Villasin Escalante's

Pigeon Peas, Pork and Jackfruit Soup
(Kadyos, Baboy at Langka)

shared by Antonio Escalante

Serves 8 to 10

This is the homecoming dish for my siblings and I. It's something that we just love and look forward to eating, and we always requested for it each time we went home; in my case, from Manila where I studied and worked for a certain time. Back then, I made it a point to return to my family's home town as often as I could. Whenever I stepped off the plane at Bacolod, I would be excited. I still get that feeling today. That's why when I fly back to Bacolod, I just get a one-way ticket because I know I'll just end up extending my stay anyway.

2 cups pigeon peas (*kadyos*)

cooking oil, as needed

1 large white onion, peeled and chopped

1.5–2 kg pork hock

2 bundles lemon grass, ends trimmed and bruised

salt, to season

water, as needed

6 *batwan*, pounded

250 g young jackfruit (*langka*), peeled and chopped

3 red chillies, sliced thinly at a diagonal

3 green chillies, sliced thinly at a diagonal

ground black pepper, to season

1. Soak pigeon peas in cold water overnight.

2. In a pot, heat some oil and sauté onion until translucent.

3. Add pork hock, lemon grass and a little salt, then add just enough water to cover pork. Bring to the boil, then lower heat and simmer for 10 minutes. Strain and discard liquid.

4. Return pork hock and lemon grass to the pot. Fill with enough water to cover pork. Bring to the boil, then lower heat and simmer for 40 minutes, or just until pork is tender.

5. Drain pigeon peas and add to the pot. Simmer for 45 minutes.

6. Add *batwan*, jackfruit and chillies and cook, covered, for another 20 minutes.

7. Season with salt and pepper. Serve.

Tasty Tip

Batwan belongs to the same family as mangosteen. It is a fruit commonly found in Bohol and is typically used as a souring agent in cooking.

"This was something that my dad cooked whenever we returned home from our studies in Manila."

Pepe and Naty Atillo's

Ox Tail and Trotter Stew
(Balbacua)

shared by Myke Sarthou

Serves 6 to 10

This ox tail and trotter stew is the Cebuano hybrid of peanut stew (*kare-kare*) and tripe with chickpeas (*callos*). It's a dish that's so delicious, but very difficult to make. Fortunately, my mother's family had cooks back in those days, allowing us to enjoy it frequently. As it has a lot of ingredients and involves a lot of work, many people usually helped to prepare it, inevitably making it a communal activity. To this day, we prepare this dish the old-fashioned way and haven't attempted adjusting it with the use of a pressure cooker or beef stock cubes. We would still cook it over charcoal or a stovetop for long hours.

4 ox trotters, about 8 kg total

1 ox tail, about 3 kg

5-cm knob ginger, peeled and cut into strips

8 star anise

6 bay leaves

$^1/_2$ cup vegetable oil

2 heads garlic, peeled and crushed

6 medium yellow onions, peeled and minced

6 medium red capsicums (bell peppers), deseeded and diced

$^3/_4$ cup fermented black beans

$^1/_4$ cup annatto powder

$^1/_2$ cup tomato paste

2 85-g cans liver spread

1 836-g can pineapple chunks, drained

8 green chillies, cut diagonally

2 cups fried peanuts, crushed

water, as needed

salt and ground black pepper, to taste

1. Wash ox parts thoroughly. Arrange in a large pot and add just enough cold water to cover meat. Boil for 30 minutes. Discard water and rinse meat.

2. Repeat to cover meat with cold water a second time. Add ginger, star anise and bay leaves. Simmer over low heat for 8 hours or until meat is tender. Skim off any impurities that accumulate on the surface from time to time.

3. Remove meat from stock. Reserve stock. When cool enough to handle, cut meat into bite-size pieces. Discard bones. Set aside.

4. In another pot, heat oil and sauté garlic and onions until onions are translucent. Add capsicums, black beans, annatto powder, tomato paste, liver spread, pineapple chunks, chillies and peanuts. Mix well.

5. Add meat and sauté lightly. Add reserved stock and water to achieve desired soupiness. Season with salt and pepper. Simmer for 1 hour or until meat is gelatinous. Serve.

Tasty Tip

In Cebu, this dish is typically served with white corn rice (*bigas mais*), which is akin to polenta.

"Ginger and star anise give this dish a distinct flavour, while pineapple chunks add a sweet surprise."

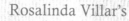

Ox Tongue Stew (Lengua Mechada)

shared by Giney Villar

Serves 6

When my mom got married, she resolved to learn how to cook. After a few false starts and some cooking lessons, she became very good at it. We had so much confidence in her cooking that whenever we tried something we liked in a restaurant or at a friend's house, we knew we could rely on her to replicate it.

The base recipe for this stew was taught by a family friend—Tito Boy Alejandrino, himself an excellent cook. His recipe has apples in it; those really ripe ones that would easily crumble in the sauce. What my mom did was to take the idea and use it in her dish. She added puréed apples and I must say, she outdid herself with her own version of this dish.

1 ox tongue, 2–3 kg

1.5 kg very ripe tomatoes

2 stalks celery

1 very ripe, large red apple, cored, peeled and chopped

¼ cup olive oil

2 Tbsp minced garlic

2 medium yellow onions, peeled and chopped

2 bay leaves

½ Tbsp whole black peppercorns

1 Tbsp sugar

2 Tbsp light soy sauce

2 Tbsp white vinegar

1 carrot, peeled and cut into cubes

1 medium red capsicum (bell pepper), deseeded and cut into cubes

1. Boil ox tongue for 15–20 minutes or until rough layer and film can be peeled off. Set aside. When cool enough to handle, peel tongue.

2. Score and boil tomatoes in a pot of water for 1 minute. Peel and set aside. Reserve 3–4 cups of the liquid used to boil tomatoes.

3. In a blender, purée boiled tomatoes, celery and apple. If mixture is too thick to blend, add some reserved liquid from boiling tomatoes. Set aside.

4. In a large pot, heat olive oil and sauté garlic until golden brown. Add onions and sauté until onions are translucent.

5. Add bay leaves, peppercorns, sugar, soy sauce and vinegar. Do not stir before bubbles start to appear.

6. Gently lay ox tongue in pot, then add puréed tomatoes, celery and apple. Add enough water reserved from boiling tomatoes to cover meat. Cook over low heat until ox tongue is tender and liquid is reduced to the consistency of sauce. Adjust seasoning to taste. If the tongue is already tender before the sauce reaches the desired consistency, remove tongue and set aside, covered, to prevent tongue from drying out. Continue to simmer liquid until desired consistency is achieved. Return tongue to pot.

7. Add carrot and cook for another 8 minutes. Add capsicum and cook for another 3 minutes. Serve.

"Whenever I wanted to eat this dish, I had to get on my mom's good side so she would prepare it for me as it is quite laborious to do."

Consolacion Fuentes's

Liver and Radish Miso Soup

shared by Cynthia Comsti

Serves 4 to 6

When we were still kids, our mom would always have us girls accompany her to the market. Saturday mornings were typically spent that way as there would be a street fair and it was the perfect time to purchase our groceries for the weekend. We rode the horse-drawn carriage (*kalesa*) and followed our mom around as she snaked through the crowds. In between small chit-chat with the vendors, she would introduce us to the different fresh produce and cuts of meat. One, which I remember, is the liver. Upon order, the vendor would wrap the item in banana leaves followed by newspaper. She would then hand it to my mom who in turn, would drop it in our *bayong*, a large bag made of palm leaves. At that point, I knew that this dish would be served. And it usually made me very excited!

cooking oil, as needed

4 cloves garlic, peeled and minced

1 medium white onion, peeled and thinly sliced

1 medium tomato, chopped

1 cup yellow miso paste

250 g pork, cut into small cubes

6 cups rice wash

2 medium radishes, peeled and cut into small cubes

500 g pork liver, cut into small cubes

1 Tbsp white vinegar

1 tsp salt

1/2 tsp sugar

1. In a pan, heat some oil. Add garlic and sauté until light brown. Add onion, tomato and miso paste and cook until soft onion is soft.

2. Add pork and sauté for a minute. Add rice wash. Lower heat and simmer until pork is tender.

3. Add radishes and cook until tender.

4. Add liver, vinegar, salt and sugar and cook over low heat for about 7 minutes or until liver is cooked through. Serve.

"Whenever my mom served this dish, she would serve it with something fried, usually fish."

Rosalinda Villar's

Stewed Pork Knuckle
(Estofadong Pata)

shared by Giney Villar

Serves 6

This is a childhood favourite—very much so that whenever my mom rang the dinner bell, my sisters Gizelle, Marjorie and I would scramble to get down the stairs as the first one to get to the table would get the nicest, thickest cut of pork knuckle.

Our family's stewed pork knuckle (*estofado*) is actually a cross between two pork stews, the Chinese-influenced *humba* and the Iberian-influenced *estofado*. Traditional *humba* uses pork belly (*liempo*) while *estofado* uses pork knuckle (*pata*). But our family prefers to cook the dish with knuckle for the mouthfeel and appearance. And while both have a sweet soy-based sauce, the sidings differ. *Humba* is served with generous portions of fried Cardava banana (*saba*) and peanuts while *estofado* is commonly served with fried sweet potato and bread.

1.5 kg pork knuckle, cut into 4-cm pieces

$6^1/_2$ cups water

1 cup packed brown sugar

3 shallots, peeled and minced

2 Tbsp garlic, peeled and minced

2.5-cm knob ginger, peeled and thinly sliced

$^1/_2$ cup pigeon peas (*kadios*), boiled

$^1/_2$ cup light soy sauce

1 stick cinnamon bark

2 star anise

2–3 Tbsp banana blossoms

3–4 Cardava bananas (*saba*), peeled and sliced lengthways

$^1/_2$ cup dry-roasted peanuts

spring onions, for garnish

1. Place pork knuckle in a braising pan with $2^1/_2$ cups water. Bring to the boil, then discard liquid. Set aside.

2. In a pot, caramelise brown sugar. Add pork knuckle, remaining water, shallots, garlic, ginger, pigeon peas, soy sauce, cinnamon, star anise and banana blossoms. Bring to the boil.

3. When water is boiling, lower heat and simmer until meat is tender and liquid is reduced to the consistency of sauce. Do not stir the contents around too much as the meat might fall off the bones.

4. In a shallow pan, fry bananas until golden brown. Place on paper towels to remove excess oil.

5. To serve, place meat on a serving platter. Pour sauce over and top with fried bananas, peanuts and spring onions.

"This is one of the dishes my mom has perfected. I even remember thinking then, that I could eat it every day for a year!"

Buenaventura dela Fuente's

Beef Shank Soup (Pochero)

shared by Dedet dela Fuente

Serves 6

Lolo Turing, as we fondly call him, isn't my grandfather but my dad. I call him as such because that is what my daughters call him. Since he grew up in Bulacan, he feasted on meats most of his life. He only started eating seafood when he married my mom who is from Parañaque. Beef shank soup is one of his favourite dishes, that's why my mother had to learn the recipe from my paternal grandmother, Lola Gelang, so that when he craved for it, she could easily cook a big batch. And just how much did my dad love this dish? Well, it always made Sunday lunches! This dish was always served during the weekend also because it had everything in it—beef, chicken and pork, in the form of chorizo, and vegetables.

1 kg beef shank, cut into cubes

¹/₄ tsp whole black peppercorns

water, as needed

2 medium sweet potatoes, peeled and cut into cubes

2 medium potatoes, peeled and cubed

1 small head cabbage, chopped

3 small heads Chinese cabbage, chopped

1 head garlic, peeled and minced

1 white onion, peeled and chopped

500 g chicken, cut into serving pieces

1 400-g can chickpeas, drained

250 g green beans, trimmed and chopped

2 pieces Spanish chorizo, thinly sliced

2 cups tomato sauce

3 Cardava bananas (*saba*)

Eggplant Salad

3 medium eggplants

1 head garlic, peeled and minced

1 white onion, peeled and minced

¹/₄ cup white vinegar

salt and ground black pepper, to taste

1. Place beef and peppercorns in a pot. Add just enough water to cover beef. Bring to the boil and continue cooking for about 1 hour 30 minutes or until beef is almost tender. Skim off any impurities that accumulate on the surface of stock from time to time.

2. Add sweet potatoes and potatoes. Cook until tender.

3. Add cabbages and cook until wilted. Strain pot and reserve liquid.

4. In a pan, sauté garlic, onion and chicken until chicken is cooked.

5. Add chickpeas, green beans and chorizo. Sauté.

6. Add cooked beef and vegetables along with tomato sauce. Bring to the boil.

7. To make eggplant salad, grill eggplants until softened. Peel off and discard skin. Chop and place in a bowl with garlic and onion. Add vinegar and mix. Season with salt and pepper.

8. To make boiled bananas, boil bananas in a pot of water for 15–20 minutes until bananas are soft. Drain and leave to cool slightly. Peel and halve lengthways.

9. Serve stew with eggplant salad, boiled bananas and reserved broth.

"This recipe comes with an eggplant salad (ensaladang talong), which I really like, and boiled bananas, which all went to Lolo Turing because he likes them."

Apung Bito's

Pork, Chicken and Beef in Clear Broth (Nilagang Pasko)

shared by Namee Jorolan

Serves 6

This version of beef stew with clear broth (*nilaga*) has pork, chicken and beef flavours unlike other dishes which only have a single origin in terms of flavour. Thus, all the holiday ingredients were usually dedicated to this dish. When my maternal grandfather used to prepare it, he would put together a big stockpot of gelatinous bone marrow (*bulalo*), chicken and fatty pork belly days before Christmas. He used the hogs that he himself raised as he was very particular about the ingredients used, believing that these guarantee the flavour of both the meat and the broth. At times, he also added Chorizo de Bilbao from Spain. The longstanding traditional of preparing this family holiday dish is continued by my mom today. She would cook a big batch of it as early as December 23.

1 kg beef shin or shank, cut into large chunks

1 kg pork kneecap

1 ham bone

2 medium white onions, peeled and chopped

1 tsp freshly ground black pepper

water, as needed

1 whole chicken, cut into pieces

1 kg pork belly, cut into 2.5-cm thick strips

whole black peppercorns and rock salt, to season

4 medium potatoes, peeled and quartered

3 ears sweet corn, husks removed and cut into thirds

1 small can chickpeas, drained

1 head white cabbage, chopped

1 head Chinese cabbage, chopped

250 g green beans, trimmed and chopped

1 stalk leek, sliced

1. In a deep stockpot, place beef shin or shank, kneecap, ham bone, onions and ground pepper. Add enough water to cover ingredients. Bring to the boil and cook for about 30 minutes. Skim off any impurities that accumulate on the surface from time to time.

2. Add chicken, including neck and feet. Boil for another 15 minutes. Repeat to skim off any impurities that accumulate on the surface from time to time.

3. Add pork belly. Season with whole peppercorns and rock salt. Lower heat and simmer until meats are almost tender.

4. Add potatoes, sweet corn and chickpeas. Cook until potatoes are tender.

5. Add cabbages, green beans and leek and cook just until cabbage is just slightly wilted. Serve.

"Whenever my mom made this, she would wrap the vegetables tightly with cloth, so they wouldn't dissolve into the broth."

Fish &
Seafood

Estanislawa Abergas's

Drunken Prawns
(Nilasing na Hipon)

shared by Aileen Anastacio

Serves 4

In Bulacan, where my maternal grandmother used to live, people would go to the wet market early in the morning to buy fresh live prawns, which they would serve for the day's lunch. Whenever I was at my Lola Ine's house and I found out that they would be serving this dish, I would go straight to the kitchen to watch how they prepared it. It just amazed me to see how the jumping prawns would mellow down and turn pink after being doused with gin. Witnessing that made me all the more excited to taste it. And as children, we were allowed to do so even if there was a pretty evident alcohol flavour. Now, whenever we have it for Sunday lunch over at my house, my daughter Sabrina can't wait to have her share of the prawns.

500 g fresh large prawns, trimmed

2 cups gin

2 tsp salt

$1/2$ tsp ground black pepper

$1^1/2$ cups cornflour (cornstarch)

cooking oil, as needed

1. Place prawns in a deep dish or bowl. Add gin and allow to marinate for at least 30 minutes.

2. Drain prawns. Season with salt and pepper. Toss to mix well.

3. Toss prawns in cornflour. Do this in batches. Shake off excess.

4. Heat oil in a pan and deep-fry prawns in small batches for about 3 minutes or until crisp and golden. Place on paper towels to drain excess oil. Serve.

Tasty Tip

Serve with sweet chilli sauce or a condiment made of white vinegar, light soy sauce and chopped onion, garlic and red bird's eye chilli.

"I remember my Lola Ine serving her home-made sweet and sour sauce as a condiment for this dish."

Paula Esconda Mesina's

Prawns with Coconut Milk and Bilimbi Fruit

shared by Divine Enya Mesina

Serves 4

This dish has already seen so many transformations. The first time I had it was when my cousin brought it as a homecoming gift (*pasalubong*) from my mother's home town of San Pablo, Laguna. It was placed in a large glass jar and the shrimps were small freshwater ones called *tagunton*. When my mother, Paula, cooked it for us at home, she used medium-size white prawns (*swahe*) because it could be bought by the pile and were usually cheaper than other types of prawns. Even then, it was not an everyday dish for my family because buying prawns still made a dent in the family's finances. We had it only occasionally when my father or brother got their salaries.

2 Tbsp cooking oil

5-cm knob ginger, peeled and thinly sliced

3 Tbsp chopped garlic

1 medium white onion, peeled and chopped

1 kg large prawns (shrimps), trimmed

3 cups coconut cream

4 cups bilimbi fruit (*kamias*), washed and sliced

salt and ground black pepper, to season

1 bundle spring onion, sliced diagonally

3 green chillies, thinly sliced

2–3 bird's eye chillies, chopped

1. In a pan over medium high heat, heat oil and sauté ginger for about 2 minutes or until slightly dark brown at the edges.

2. Add garlic and sauté for a couple of minutes. Add onion and cook for another 3 minutes.

3. Add prawns and stir until they start to turn bright orange.

4. Add coconut cream and bring to a simmer, stirring constantly to prevent coconut cream from curdling.

5. Add bilimbi fruit. Cover and cook for 5 minutes.

6. Season with salt and pepper. Add spring onion and green chillies. Stir.

7. Add bird's eye chilli and stir. Serve.

Tasty Tip

Bilimbi fruit, also known as *kamias* in the Philippines, is a very juicy and extremely sour bright green fruit.

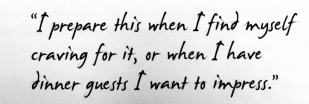

"I prepare this when I find myself craving for it, or when I have dinner guests I want to impress."

Antonia del Valle Ortega's

Shrimp Royale

shared by Gwen Jacinto-Cariño

Serves 6 to 8

My family lived in Grace Park, Caloocan until I was in grade three. And while our house and neighbourhood were conducive to safe and fun playing, I clearly remember intentionally missing playtime whenever I discovered that my mom would be cooking my grandmother's shrimp dish for supper. I would stay in the kitchen and wait until they were done so I could taste the dish right away, even before it was served. That's how much I liked this dish. So did my dad and my sisters. My father, Naning, also had his own version of this dish, made with the inclusion of boiled quail eggs.

2 Tbsp unsalted butter

500 g shrimps, peeled and deveined

$^{1}/_{2}$ cup canned whole button mushrooms, drained and sliced in half

2–3 Tbsp freshly-squeezed calamansi lime juice

$^{1}/_{4}$ cup frozen sweet peas

1 tsp cornflour (cornstarch), mixed with $^{1}/_{4}$ cup water

$^{1}/_{4}$ cup roasted cashew nuts

1 dozen quail eggs, hard-boiled and peeled (optional)

salt and ground black pepper, to taste

1. In a medium pan, heat butter and sauté shrimps. When shrimps are half-cooked, add mushrooms.
2. Add calamansi lime juice and cook for 3 minutes.
3. Add sweet peas and cornflour slurry and let boil.
4. Add cashew nuts and quail eggs, if using.
5. Season with salt and pepper. Serve with rice.

"I would just hang out in the kitchen and with an eagle eye, wait for the cooks to finish prepping the dish so I could have a taste of it."

Vicente Mercado's

Chilli Crabs and Prawns

shared by Chona Ayson

Serves 4 to 6

My grandfather Vicente owned a fish pond in Sasmuan, Pampanga and those who leased it often dropped off bucket loads of crabs and prawns at our doorstep as a gratuity. And this is how the freshly-caught produce would usually end up on our table, or as seafood stew in peanut sauce (*kare-kareng dagat*). In any case, they are both delicious ways of cooking seafood.

Since then, this dish has become my mother's specialty, one that has never missed an occasion. Be it a family member's birthday, the neighbourhood party (*barrio fiesta*) or Christmas, her chilli crabs and prawns would always be in attendance. And thankfully so, because we like it a lot! It's the type of dish that requires you to use clean, bare hands to eat and leads you to licking your fingers after!

3 large crabs, scrubbed clean

cooking oil, as needed

2.5-cm knob ginger, peeled and halved lengthwise

3 cloves garlic, peeled and chopped

1 big white onion, peeled and diced

2 Tbsp Worcestershire sauce

³/₄ cup spicy ketchup

1 Tbsp white sugar

salt and ground black pepper, to taste

500 g large fresh prawns, trimmed

3 stalks leek, cut into thin strips

1. In a pot, place whole crabs and enough water to cover them. Set on medium heat and boil for 20 minutes or until fully cooked. Remove crabs and set aside to cool before cutting in half. Reserve liquid.

2. In a deep pan, heat some oil and sauté ginger, garlic and onion until onion is translucent.

3. Add crabs and sauté lightly.

4. Add 2 cups reserved liquid, Worcestershire sauce, ketchup, sugar, salt and pepper. Cover and bring to the boil.

5. Add prawns. When prawns are cooked, add leeks. Stir for a minute, then remove from heat. Serve.

"Sometimes, my mother would make more than the usual serving so that we would have leftovers to take home."

Juanita Sarthou's

Whole Fish Braised in Coconut Milk

shared by Myke Sarthou

Serves 4 to 6

Everybody in my family cooks, but not to the same degree as my grandmother did. She was from Naga, Bicol and whenever she made this dish, she always had a story about coconut milk to tell. Once, she told me that she would just have plain coconut milk to go with her rice and that would already be her meal. With this particular dish, she would dice the tomatoes and mash it with her hands along with the ginger and onions. Since the fish is braised, the bottom part might be cooked, but the top might not be and so it sometimes became my job to see that this did not happen. It's a very social dish as the whole family would feast on one big fish.

banana leaves

1 whole crimson snapper (*maya-maya*) or jack fish (*talakitok*), about 1.2 kg

salt, to season

10 ripe tomatoes, diced

2 medium red onions, peeled and minced

7.5-cm knob ginger, peeled and finely minced

2 green chillies or 1 bird's eye chilli, sliced diagonally

freshly-squeezed coconut milk from 3 grated coconuts

1. Line a big wok with banana leaves.

2. Clean the fish and score diagonally. Season the cavity with salt and place on top of banana leaves.

3. Place tomatoes, onions, ginger and chillies in a bowl and sprinkle with salt. Mash everything with clean hands and place over fish.

4. Gently pour coconut milk over fish.

5. Place wok over low heat and baste fish occasionally until it is fully cooked and the coconut milk has reduced by half. Turn fish over and cook for a few more minutes. Do not allow the coconut milk to boil or it will split. Serve.

Tasty Tip

This dish tastes better with reheating as more coconut oil would be released each time.

"I once cooked this for the 70th birthday of a client. One of her daughters loved it so much that she ordered it for herself a week after."

Cynthia Comsti's
Fish in Guava Soup
(Sinigang sa Bayabas)

shared by Angelo Comsti

Serves 4 to 6

Many Filipino households consider *sinigang* (sour soup) a dining table staple. Ours is no different. It shows up at least thrice a month. And since my mom cooks it in big batches, it sometimes does a comeback during the week. The soup, soured with unripe tamarind and cooked with pork belly, is the one that is usually prepared. But what I really like is the soup flavoured with guava and cooked with milkfish belly. I would often have heaps of rice whenever my mom serves that.

It's my comfort food of choice, the type that would have me spontaneously drive to a restaurant (when I'm too lazy to cook), order it to go and selfishly indulge in it at home —at times, with my feet up. Comfort, indeed.

cooking oil, as needed

1 medium white onion, peeled and sliced

6 tomatoes, chopped

1 small fresh banana blossom, sliced

8 medium ripe guavas, peeled

6 cups rice wash

6 pieces milkfish (*bangus*) belly fillets

1 bunch water spinach (*kangkong*)

1 tsp salt

fish sauce, to taste

1. In a pot, heat oil and sauté onion and tomatoes until onion is translucent. Add banana blossom and guavas and cook until tender.

2. Pour in rice wash and let boil.

3. Add milkfish belly as soon as water comes to a rapid boil. Lower heat to a simmer.

4. When fish is cooked, add water spinach and salt. Cook for another 5 minutes. Adjust taste with fish sauce. Serve.

Tasty Tip
You can also add eggplant to the mix. Simply slice and add it in along with the water spinach and banana blossom.

"I love guava in its different forms —juice, jam, bars or as is, with a sprinkling of salt. Whenever this is served, I find myself staying longer than usual at the dining table."

Florentino Mesina's

Sour Soup with Taro and Fried Fish
(Sinigang na Gabi at Pritong Bangus)

shared by Divine Enya Mesina

Serves 4

Between my parents, my father was the better cook. Mang Tino, as he was called by close friends, was the king of the kitchen and he often prepared our meals. Of his dishes, this is the one that has left quite a mark on me. I was 12 years old when he passed away and my mom Paula Esconda continued to cook it long after his passing, but hers just didn't compare to what my father did.

I haven't tasted this dish anywhere else and I don't know if this is a dish commonly served in his province of Cabiao, Nueva Ecija. This dish is really sour, the broth is velvety due to the taro, and there's an added crunch because of the fried fish. According to my brother Ernesto, you have to cook the taro in a separate pot because if you cook it in the sour broth, it won't be as tender.

250 g fresh unripe tamarind fruit, peeled

$3^1/_2$–$4^1/_2$ cups water

1 large milkfish (*bangus*), about 1 kg, cut into 4 pieces

salt, to season

cooking oil, as needed

1 Tbsp minced garlic

1 medium yellow onion, peeled and chopped

2 Tbsp shrimp paste (*bagoong*)

1 kg small taro, peeled, quartered and boiled until tender

1. In a small pot, boil unripe tamarind fruit in $1^1/_2$ cups water until tender. Scoop out tamarind and place in a strainer over the pot. Crush and press out as much juice from the tamarind as possible. Discard solids. Set liquid aside.

2. Season fish with salt. Heat some oil and fry fish until cooked. Place on paper towels to drain excess oil. Set aside.

3. In a large pot, heat some oil and sauté garlic and onion for about 3 minutes. Add shrimp paste and cook for 5 minutes. Add 2–3 cups water and bring to the boil. Lower heat and simmer for a couple minutes more.

4. Add boiled taro and tamarind liquid. Stir. Add fried milkfish and simmer for 5 minutes. Serve.

Tasty Tip

To make the broth rich and slightly thick, crush a few pieces of the taro and stir into the soup.

"A typical Filipino meal usually
includes a soup and something fried.
Well, this has both, two-in-one."

Lorna Lombos-dela Fuentes's

Stuffed Milkfish
(Rellenong Bangus)

shared by Dedet dela Fuente

Serves 4 to 6

Both my parents are lawyers. In fact, my mom used to be the presiding justice of the Court of Appeals, and they wanted me to be a lawyer as well. But I never wanted to be one. My parents were career-driven and I, as an only child, experienced what it was like not having them around most of the time. Hence, having the same profession never appealed to me.

Despite how busy my mother was, she would still make up for lost time in the weekends by taking on the role of a homemaker. She would either knit me a sweater or prepare food for the family. Of all her dishes, this is the one I treasure the most.

2 milkfish (*bangus*), about 1 kg altogether, fish meat separated from cavity, backbones removed leaving fish intact

cooking oil, as needed

3 medium potatoes, peeled and chopped

1 head garlic, peeled and minced

1 small white onion, peeled and minced

6 pieces water chestnuts, peeled and minced

$^1/_4$ cup raisins

salt and ground black pepper, to season

2 medium hard-boiled eggs, peeled

1. In a large pot, boil fish meat in water for about 12 minutes until fully cooked. Drain and set aside to cool. When cool enough to handle, pick out meat and discard bones. Set cooked fish meat aside.

2. In a pan over medium heat, heat oil and sauté potatoes until tender. Add garlic, onion, chestnuts, raisins and fish meat. Mix and season with salt and pepper. Transfer to a bowl and let cool.

3. Preheat oven to 180°C (350°F).

4. Using a spoon, stuff each fish with some potato mixture and a hard-boiled egg.

5. Place stuffed fish on a lined baking tray and bake for 30 minutes. Serve.

Tasty Tip

Instead of chicken eggs, you can use quail eggs, which are easier to stuff into the fish.

"When it comes to food, my mother always has a version of our favourite dishes and she makes sure to put her own signature style on each one."

Dioscora de Guzman's

Milkfish Braised in Fermented Soy Bean and Ginger (Tochong Bangus)

shared by Jun Jun de Guzman

Serves 6 to 8

My mother's family—the Javiers—came from Navotas. It was a fishing town before as there was a fishing port in the area. As such, many residents in the city got to enjoy seafood on a daily basis. This dish was prepared whenever there was a good catch of milkfish. And by good, I mean they were big!

This recipe calls for fish of a certain size and weight—at least one kilo per piece—because the serving portions should be huge. It carries the distinct taste of garlic, ginger and fermented soy beans, which is where the saltiness of the dish comes from. This dish drives you to eat heaps of rice. The broth alone can stand as a satisfying viand. The reason why it's fried first before braising is to keep the fish intact.

2 milkfish (*bangus*), about 1 kg altogether, cut into 2.5-cm thick steaks

salt and ground black pepper, to season

$^1/_2$ cup canola oil

$^1/_2$ cup plain (all-purpose) flour

1 head garlic, peeled and finely minced

3 medium white onions, peeled and finely chopped

13-cm knob ginger, peeled and sliced into matchsticks

$^1/_4$ cup water

$^1/_2$ cube fermented soy beans (*taure*), mashed

3 Tbsp white vinegar

$^1/_2$ tsp light soy sauce

2 Tbsp fish sauce

1. Season milkfish with salt and pepper.

2. In a pan, heat oil. Dredge each piece with flour, then pan-fry until browned on both sides. Remove and place on paper towels to drain excess oil. Set aside.

3. In the same pan, sauté garlic, onions and ginger. Cook until onions are translucent.

4. Add water and fermented soy beans. Let boil.

5. Add vinegar, soy sauce and fish sauce. Let boil and simmer for 5 minutes.

6. Return fried milkfish to pan and cook for another 15–20 minutes over low heat. Serve.

"My mom never passed on her recipes.
And so for our family to preserve them,
we had to recreate the dishes according to
how we remember them by taste."

Angelita Virrey Bernardo's

Calamari in Black Ink Sauce

shared by Arnold Bernardo

Serves 6

My mom used to have stacks of recipes on the shelf. We often found her snipping newspapers or taking the labels off canned goods, pasting the recipes on scrap pieces of paper, then fastening them all up in folders. It became her favourite pastime. And she managed to do this even after having to juggle two jobs and cooking dinner for the whole family daily. She always made time for what she wanted to do and this inspired me to do the same. I believe this is one trait I am proud to have inherited from her. And along with it, I took this recipe and used it to join cooking contests. It received rave reviews and eventually, I got my big break in the business—all thanks to my mom.

1 kg small squid (calamari)

1 cup minced garlic

1 cup lemon-lime soda

1 tsp freshly ground black pepper

$^1/_2$ tsp salt

1 tsp liquid seasoning

$^1/_2$ cup unsalted butter

1. Clean squid. Cut off the eyes and beak and remove the spine. Leave the ink sac intact.

2. In a bowl, mix together $^1/_2$ cup garlic, lemon-lime soda, pepper, salt and liquid seasoning. Add squid and leave to marinate for 30 minutes.

3. In a pan, heat butter and sauté remaining garlic until slightly brown.

4. Add squid, including marinade. Cook for 5 minutes or until squid has shrunk. Remove squid. Continue cooking mixture until it is reduced and has the consistency of sauce.

5. Return squid to the pan and sauté to heat through. Serve.

Tasty Tip

This can be a base recipe for paella with squid ink.
Prepare the dish as directed above, then set the squid aside and cook the rice in the liquid.

"I liked this dish so much when I was young that I couldn't have squid served to me any other way!"

Dioscora de Guzman's

Stuffed Squid (Batuta)

shared by Jun Jun de Guzman

Serves 4 to 6

I didn't live with my biological parents when I was growing up. My uncle Ben and Aunt Luring adopted me when I was just six months old. Nevertheless, one thing I learned from my mom was cooking. I learned simply by watching her, especially those dishes we enjoyed eating like this one. This is something I would request her to prepare whenever we visited. It's very aromatic. In fact, the smell hits you as soon as you enter the house.

For this dish to taste good, the squid has to be really fresh as only a very small amount of spices and flavouring is used in the stuffing. It's really the pronounced flavour of the squid that we aim to enjoy, complimented by the pork and shrimp.

1 kg small to medium squid
(*calamari*)

¹/₄ cup corn oil

1 Tbsp finely minced garlic

¹/₄ cup finely chopped white onions

200 g minced pork

200 g shrimp, peeled, deveined and finely chopped

fish sauce, to season

freshly ground black pepper,
to season

¹/₄ cup water

light soy sauce, to season

1. Clean squid. Pull off and discard the head with the ink sac and tentacles. Remove and discard the spine.

2. In a pan, heat oil and sauté garlic and onions until onions are translucent. Add minced pork and prawns. Cook well. Season with fish sauce and pepper. Set aside to cool.

3. Stuff squid tubes with pork and shrimp mixture, then secure with toothpicks. Lay squid in a deep pan and cook over medium heat until juices are released.

4. Add water and let boil. Adjust seasoning with fish sauce, soy sauce and pepper. Remove toothpicks before serving.

Tasty Tip

Save the tentacles and include them in the stuffing by finely chopping and adding to the pan along with the shrimp.

"One way to find out
if someone is really from
Navotas is by asking if he eats
batuta (literally policeman's club).
Those who are not familiar with the
dish will think you're referring to the
policeman's club or cudgel!"

Sweets & Desserts

Ditas Rodrigo Sevilla's

Bulacan Custard (Pinaso)

shared by Pixie Sevilla

Serves 8 to 10

This recipe has already spanned so many lifetimes. My maternal grandmother grew up with it. So did my mom. And I remember having it the first time when I was 3 years old. Today, it is served when we have our Sunday lunches at my grandmother's house, not every week, but at least twice a month when my grandmother is not busy fulfilling church responsibilities. She told me the process of making this custard, but she doesn't remember the measurements anymore. It's a good thing my mom, Ditas, took note of the portions before and so she simply provided the numbers for me. Now, I'm hoping to pass it on to my daughter who has a liking for sweets.

3 cups evaporated milk

$3/4$ cup white sugar

1 cup ground butter cookies

5 large eggs

juice of 1 lime

1. In a bowl, combine evaporated milk, $1/2$ cup sugar, ground butter cookies and eggs. Mix well.

2. Transfer mixture to a pot. Stir continuously over low heat until mixture is thick.

3. Add lime juice and mix, then remove from heat.

4. Pour mixture into a shallow bowl. Let cool for at least 15 minutes to slightly set.

5. Sprinkle remaining sugar over setting mixture and caramelise by placing in a salamander or using a kitchen torch. Serve.

"This is Bulacan's version of a crème brûlée with some minor differences. Crème brûlée is set and smooth, while this one is like a very thick cream with cookie crumbs."

Urbana Victorino's

Coconut Pralines (Bukayo)

shared by Cynthia Comsti

Makes about 50 pieces

Of the desserts my maternal grandmother Urbana, Lelang Banang to many, prepared for my family's daily meals and for entertaining visitors, this is one of the few that I learned how to make. I found it really delicious and that's why I made sure to watch her do it each time so that I could prepare it on my own later on. She used a copper pan to make it and she would just dump all the ingredients in it, mix gently, then heat over a low fire. Once cooked and cooled, she let me form them with her copper *polvoron* (Spanish shortbread) mould and coat them with sugar. I was fortunate to inherit not only the recipe but also the pan she cooked this dessert in.

2 young coconuts, grated

zest of 2 limes, finely chopped

2 egg yolks, beaten

1¼ cups condensed milk

white sugar, for coating

1. In a large pan, combine grated coconut, lime zest and egg yolks. Mix well.

2. Gradually stir in condensed milk. Place pan over low heat. Stir until mixture thickens. Set aside to cool.

3. Shape mixture into individual serving pieces using a *polvoron* mould, cookie mould or measuring spoon.

4. Gently roll in sugar. Serve or store in an airtight container in the refrigerator for up to 2 weeks.

Tasty Tip

As a variation to this recipe, replace the lime zest with finely chopped jackfruit.

"Before, everything was made from scratch. The coconuts, for example, were grated by hand. The men would sit on wooden stools with a grater attached at one end, then work on the coconuts to get all the meat out."

Amparo Aguas Mercado's

Petito Cookies

shared by Chona Ayson

Makes about 24 cookies

My maternal grandmother, Lola Paring, used to buy this delicacy from another grandma even if she knew how to make it and would often bake it herself. I had no idea that she made it often during her baking days in the 1940s until the 1960s. I never got to taste Lola Paring's *petitos* because she stopped making them before I was born. Being a Pampanga delicacy and a favourite after meal snack, I had my share of these bite-sized cookies from the ones sold at the stores. Apparently, it was originally made with almonds and eventually localised using cashews. I used to have this for dessert or as an afternoon snack every time we had guests from Manila, and during special occasions such as fiestas and Christmas.

$1^1/_4$ cups toasted cashew nuts, finely chopped + $^1/_4$ cup raw cashew nuts, finely sliced

3 Tbsp butter, softened

1 large egg, yolk and white separated

$^1/_3$ cup + 1 Tbsp white sugar

1 Tbsp water

1. Preheat oven to 160°C (325°F).

2. In a bowl, using a fork or pastry cutter, mix toasted cashew nuts with butter until clumpy.

3. In a separate bowl, beat egg white with a whisk. Gradually add sugar and continue beating until mixture is thick. Fold into nut mixture and mix well.

4. Spoon mixture into mini paper cupcake liners until half full. Arrange 5-cm apart on a baking tray.

5. Beat egg yolk with 1 Tbsp water to make an egg wash. Brush the top of each cookie with egg wash, then top with a slice of raw cashew.

6. Bake for 20–24 minutes or until light brown. Remove from oven and place on a wire rack to cool before serving.

"Petito cookies are very similar to another Pampanga specialty—crisantes, a nutty pastry made with ground cashews and shaped like a half-moon."

Rosalinda Villar's

Christmas Cheese Balls

shared by Giney Villar

Makes about 27 balls

Like many young middle-class wives in her generation, my mom took up baking lessons. And as the eldest child, I became her assistant. My tasks included sifting flour, scraping bowls and tasting the batter before it was baked. During special occasions like birthdays and Christmas, she would leaf through magazines, books and her notes, and experiment with something new to pair with our traditional fare. This recipe was one of those Christmas discoveries, which we ended up liking a lot.

1¹/₂ cups plain (all-purpose) flour

1 tsp baking soda

1 tsp salt

113 g unsalted butter, softened + more for brushing

1 tsp finely chopped lime zest

1 egg

1 egg yolk

¹/₄ cup white sugar

¹/₂ cup grated Edam cheese (*queso de bola*)

1. In a bowl, sift together flour, baking soda and salt.

2. In another bowl and using an electric mixer, cream butter and lime zest until light and fluffy.

3. Add egg, egg yolk and sugar to butter mixture, mixing after every addition.

4. Add sifted ingredients and mix until combined.

5. Fold in grated cheese. Cover bowl and refrigerate for 10 minutes.

6. Remove batter from refrigerator. Using a measuring spoon to keep the balls to a uniform size, scoop dough and form into balls. Place on a plate and refrigerate for another 10 minutes.

7. Preheat oven to 180°C (350°F).

8. Arrange balls slightly apart on a lined baking tray. Brush with melted butter and bake for 15 minutes. Place cheese balls on a wire rack to cool.

9. Serve or store in an airtight container in a cool, dry place for up to 2 weeks.

"At our home, guests who arrived early for Christmas dinner were given these and hot chocolate to snack on."

Medy Enriquez Rodrigo's

Spanish Cream

shared by Pixie Sevilla

Serves 4 to 6

My grandmother liked preparing *pinaso* (page 110), which is like a loose crème brûlée, but her sisters, all 10 of them, favoured Spanish cream. The Enriquezes was a very affluent Spanish family in Bulacan who loved and lived to eat. If you go to their provincial home, you would still see the first version of a refrigerator. It looks like a water tank and they used to put a block of ice either at the top or the bottom of it to keep the food cool and well preserved. Not many families had such an appliance and luxury in those days. And it's great that they were able to preserve it as well as some recipes, so we can continue to pass them on for generations to come.

1 cup warm milk

3 Tbsp unflavoured gelatin powder

¹/₄ tsp salt

³/₄ cup white sugar

3 large eggs, yolks and whites separated

¹/₂ cup cold water

1 tsp vanilla extract

1 cup brown sugar

¹/₂ cup hot water

1. In a bowl, pour in milk. Sprinkle gelatin powder on milk and set aside for 5 minutes.

2. Add salt, white sugar and egg yolks and mix well. Fit bowl over a larger pot filled with simmering water and cook stirring until mixture thickens and coats the back of a spoon.

3. Stir in vanilla extract.

4. In another bowl, using an electric mixer, beat egg whites until stiff peaks form. Fold this into egg yolk mixture.

5. Spoon mixture into 4–6 ramekins, glasses or bowls. Refrigerate until set.

6. Meanwhile, place brown sugar in a pan over low to medium heat until caramelised. Add hot water and stir until fully incorporated.

7. Serve Spanish cream with caramel sauce.

"Spanish cream is similar to canonigo,
Spain's version of the French dessert
île flottante, but it's not as light."

Leonila Felipe's

Sweet Beans

shared by Maria Carmina Felipe

Serves 6

I cooked this dessert thrice, but it didn't come out exactly the way Nanay Noneng, my mother-in-law, cooks it. I always make the mistake of overcooking the beans. She tells me that the secret is to cook the beans over low heat for a long time, covered and barely stirred. I was guilty of not doing any of these three essential steps before. Now I manage to get the beans tasting great, but still not quite perfect like Nanay's.

1 Tbsp baking soda

water, as needed

500 g white beans

4 cups white sugar

$^1/_2$ tsp vanilla extract

1. In a big bowl, dissolve baking soda in 5 cups water. Add beans and leave to soak overnight.

2. Drain and wash beans thoroughly at least twice. Place in a pot and cover with water. Boil over low heat for 30–45 minutes or until beans are tender.

3. Meanwhile, place sugar in a pan over low to medium heat until caramelised. Add 2 cups water and bring to the boil. Lower heat and simmer for about 15 minutes, without stirring, until mixture is slightly thick.

4. Add beans and vanilla extract. Remove from heat. Mix well. Leave to cool before serving.

"The first time I tried this was when Leo, my husband, was still courting me. He brought over a bottle of these freshly-cooked beans that his mother had made."

Urbana Victorino's

Purple Yam Jam
(Halayang Ube)

shared by Maria Carmina Felipe

Serves 6

Lelang Banang, my maternal grandmother, would always cap off a meal with dessert, as a meal just wouldn't be complete without a sweet treat! We got so used to it that my older sister Vicky would look for something sweet after each meal, until today.

I can still recall the ingredients and the process of making this jam, but not the exact measurements, so I had to figure it out myself through a couple of trials. Back in the day, Lelang cooked it in a huge iron vat over burning coconut husks. And she would be standing over it, stirring for hours. Talk about labour of love.

1 kg purple yam (*ube*)

1 380-g can condensed milk

1 410-ml can evaporated milk

1 cup white sugar

¹/₄ cup unsalted butter + more for topping

1. Wash and brush purple yam to clean. Pat dry and slice in half. Place in a pot with enough water to cover it. Boil for about 30 minutes or until yam is tender. Drain and leave to cool.

2. Peel and grate yam into a bowl.

3. Add condensed milk, evaporated milk and sugar. Mix until well combined.

4. In a pot over medium heat, melt butter. Swirl butter to coat base of pot.

5. Add yam mixture and cook for 1 hour, stirring continuously until mixture is thick.

6. While mixture is still hot, spoon into heatproof containers. Cover top with a thin layer of melted butter. Leave to cool before serving.

Tasty Tip

Taste the yam and adjust the amount of sugar added based on the sweetness of the yam.

"Whenever we had a visitor at home, a sweet delicacy (kakanin) would be served. This was one of them."

Estanislawa Abergas's

Coconut Pudding
(Maja Blanca)

shared by Aileen Anastacio

Serves 6

My family would always drive to Bulacan every Sunday to have lunch over at our grandmother's house. And each time, a big family feast was in store for us. There was always meat, usually cooked as a soup or stew like *pochero* or with a mouth-watering thick sauce like *sarciado*, a fish or chicken dish, and to cap off the already heavy meal, a dessert. For that, fruits were typically served as the more special varieties were reserved for the afternoon, when we indulged on stuff like corn and sticky rice in coconut milk (*ginataang mais*), fried banana spring rolls (*turon*) or this coconut pudding (*maja blanca*). Those were good times as Lola Ine fed us well.

2 cups coconut milk

$^3/_4$ cup sugar

$^1/_3$ cup water

$^2/_3$ cup cornflour (cornstarch)

half the content of a 425-g can corn kernels, drained

$^1/_2$ cup toasted desiccated coconut, to garnish

1. Grease two 18 x 13-cm rectangular baking dishes.

2. In a saucepan, bring coconut milk and sugar to a gentle simmer, stirring gently and making sure sugar is fully dissolved.

3. In a separate bowl, combine water and cornflour. Stir well to combine.

4. Once coconut milk is simmering, scoop about $^1/_2$ cup out and pour into the cornflour slurry. Using a wire whisk, stir to combine.

5. Gradually return this mixture to the simmering coconut milk. Stir continuously and cook for about 4 minutes or until mixture thickens. Take off heat.

6. Add corn kernels and mix well.

7. Pour mixture into greased dishes. Smoothen the top using an oiled spatula or spoon. Leave to cool and set. This will take 1–2 hours.

8. Garnish with toasted desiccated coconut. Slice and serve.

"Desserts like this bring back
sweet memories, like my
family's Sunday lunch feasts."

Amparo Aguas Mercado's

Fruit Salad

shared by Chona Ayson

Serves 4 to 6

This recipe has been with my family for generations now. It started with my maternal grandmother, Lola Paring, who prepared this every time there was a special occasion. My mom, Maria Lourdes Ayson, was born in 1943 and she remembers having this fruit salad already back then. The original recipe didn't include nata de coco (coconut water jelly) though. It was one of the two revisions my mom made to the recipe. The other is the use of fewer egg yolks. Lola Paring used to make it with a lot more, but it was too rich so my mom adjusted it to her liking and added evaporated milk for the same purpose, consequently ending up with a creamier fruit salad that when frozen, becomes reminiscent of ice cream in texture.

$^1/_2$ cup evaporated milk

6 large egg yolks

$1^1/_4$ cups cream

2 836-g cans fruit cocktail, drained

1 227-g pack nata de coco, drained

$^1/_2$ cup white sugar

1. In a medium saucepan over medium heat, scald evaporated milk until small bubbles start to appear around the edges.

2. Put yolks in a bowl. Gently drizzle some of the warm milk over and whisk to temper. When combined, add the rest of the milk along with the cream.

3. Add fruit cocktail, nata de coco and sugar. Stir well. Freeze for at least 2 hours before serving.

"Back in the day, egg whites were used for construction and rather than letting the egg yolks go to waste, they ended up in a lot of desserts."

Cynthia Comsti's

Lime Caramel Custard
(Dayap Leche Flan)

shared by Angelo Comsti

Serves 4 to 6

This dessert had been served at many of my family's meals. It didn't even require a special occasion for it to make an appearance on the dining table. It was just there almost every day—not because no one wanted it, but because my mom made loads of it. And it's ironic that members of the family often complained about its ubiquity, yet each one of us would still be caught enjoying a huge chunk of her velvety rich flan every time.

My mom has become quite known for her flan. Come Christmas, that's what friends and relatives would request her to give away. And she would happily do so. I can't remember an instance where she didn't give in to a request—even if it was last minute since she always has all the ingredients in stock.

3 Tbsp + 1 Tbsp white sugar

4 large eggs

1¼ cups condensed milk

¾ cup water

1 tsp grated lime zest

1. In a large oval-shaped aluminium pan, caramelise 3 Tbsp sugar over low to medium heat, moving it around with a pair of tongs to evenly distribute caramel. Once sugar turns light amber, remove from stove and set aside to harden.

2. In a bowl, beat eggs with a whisk.

3. Pour in condensed milk, water, lime zest and 1 Tbsp sugar. Stir until combined. Pass mixture through a cheesecloth lined strainer. Pour into the aluminium with hardened caramel.

4. Place in a steamer and steam over low heat until custard becomes firm. Set aside to cool.

5. To loosen flan, run a knife around the side of the pan, then invert it onto a serving plate. Serve.

Tasty Tip

To check if the flan is cooked, insert a toothpick in the centre. If it comes out clean, the flan is done.

"My mom rarely makes the flan with lime zest, but whenever she does, I make sure to indulge as I enjoy the subtle tangy taste that cuts through the sweetness of the caramel."

Dolores Quemado's

Glutinous Rice with Lye Wrapped in Banana Leaves
(Suman Bulagta)

shared by Addie Wijangco

Makes 12 pieces

Ima took care of a lot of people in the family including my mom, my older sister and I. She had been with my grandmother since she was 15 and she was with us for over 50 years until she decided to move back with her family in Tarlac. I still remember the times she picked me up from school and on the trip home, she would ask me what I wanted as an afternoon snack. I had various requests that included *halo-halo*, a shaved iced dessert that she would make from scratch, but it was this *suman* that I just couldn't get enough of. I'd even help her tie the banana leaves tightly just before she put them into a big cauldron. Then while boiling, Ima would play solitaire with a deck of cards and smoke her rolled tobacco leaves.

banana leaves, cut to get 12 sheets, each 10 x 13-cm

2¹/₄ cups glutinous or sticky (*malagkit*) rice

1 tsp lye water

1. Scald banana leaves by passing each side of the leaves directly over an open flame until glossy. Doing this will make the leaf pliable and keep it from ripping when wrapping.

2. Wash rice thrice, then soak in water for 20 minutes. Drain rice, then add lye water. Mix well.

3. Place ¹/₄ cup rice in the middle of each banana leaf. Fold 2 opposite sides of banana leaf over rice, then fold ends to enclose parcel. Secure with cooking twine.

4. Place parcels in a pot and add just enough water to cover. Place a heavy object such as a ceramic plate on top of the parcels to weigh them down. Bring to the boil. Lower heat to a simmer and cook for 45 minutes or until rice is cooked. Let cool.

5. Serve with fried coconut milk solids (*latik*), toasted desiccated coconut or plain sugar.

Tasty Tip
The lye water should be pale yellow in colour. Any darker and the rice will end up tasting bitter.

"Ima means mother in the dialect of Pampanga and Ima was like a mother because she took good care of us."

Olive Guanzon's

Pineapple Upside Down Cake

shared by Addie Wijangco

Makes one 33 x 23-cm cake

When I was a child, I didn't really know how to bake. I would be in the kitchen merely to watch my mom and oftentimes, provide harmless helping. My older sister and cousins were the ones who were made to do most of the mixing and cooking. I simply took delight in watching the process of making desserts, especially this one.

I was amazed then because it was not like other cakes which you had to frost to make it look pretty when it is out of the mould. With this cake, you just overturn the baking pan and it's pretty already and all good to eat. I remember insisting on putting the pineapple slices and cherries in the pan. I was so eager and felt so privileged that I made sure to put them in the right way.

2³/₄ cups cake flour

3 tsp baking powder

1 tsp salt

³/₄ cup unsalted butter, softened

1¹/₂ cups white sugar

4 large eggs

³/₄ cup milk

1 tsp vanilla extract

Topping

6 canned pineapple rounds, syrup in can reserved

¹/₂ cup packed brown sugar

¹/₄ cup unsalted butter, softened

3 maraschino cherries, halved

1. Prepare the topping. In a small pot, combine 1 cup reserved pineapple syrup and brown sugar. Cook, stirring constantly until mixture is thick. Remove from heat and stir in butter. Pour into an ungreased 33 x 23-cm baking pan. Arrange pineapple rounds in pan and place maraschino cherries in the middle of each slice.

2. Preheat oven to 180°C (350°F).

3. In a bowl, sift together cake flour, baking powder and salt.

4. In another bowl, using an electric mixer, beat butter and white sugar until light and fluffy. Add eggs one at a time, mixing well after each addition.

5. Add flour mixture alternately with milk, mixing well after each addition.

6. Add vanilla extract and mix well. Pour batter into prepared pan. Tap pan lightly to release any air bubbles trapped in batter.

7. Bake for 40–45 minutes or until a toothpick inserted into the middle of cake comes out clean. Place pan on a wire rack to cool.

8. To loosen cake, run a knife around the side of the pan, then invert it onto a serving plate. Serve warm.

"My kids don't like this cake because of the sourness of the pineapple, thus when I bake it, I can have it all to myself, my naturally greedy sweet tooth self!"

Amanda Makabali's

Hot Chocolate (Chocolate Batirol)

shared by Chin Gallegos

Serves 6

My childhood summers were often spent in Pampanga where I would wake up to the delicious aroma of hot chocolate. It had been a daily routine which started with peddlers dropping off bottles of fresh cow's milk at our doorstep. My grandmother would then grind cacao beans into a paste, place it inside a small pot, pour in the milk and add sugar. She would then let it boil, stirring the whole time. It's quite a workout to produce a rich and silky hot chocolate, but the reward is worth all the labour and one that's enjoyed right from the very first sip. There were days when my grandmother paired it with home-made *ensaymada*, a sweet Spanish bread snack. And then there were times when she made us eat rice with it, much like a cereal or chocolate porridge. Let's just say that I would much rather drink it than scoop it!

1 cup roasted unsalted peanuts

1 cup pure cacao paste or
8 tablea tablets

4 cups fresh carabao's (water buffalo) milk

1 cup sugar

1. Grind peanuts in a blender until smooth. Set aside.

2. In a heavy-bottom pan, combine cacao paste or tablea tablets, milk and sugar. Simmer over low heat, whisking continuously for about 20 minutes.

3. Add blended peanuts and cook for another 10 minutes. Serve warm.

Tasty Tip
Skip the step of grinding the roasted peanuts by using smooth peanut butter available in jars at the supermarket.

"This drink is traditionally prepared in a batirol, a pot used specifically for making hot chocolate."

Weights &
Measures

Quantities for this book are given in Metric and American (spoon and cup) measures. Standard spoon and cup measurements used are: 1 teaspoon = 5 ml, 1 tablespoon = 15 ml, 1 cup = 250 ml. All measures are level unless otherwise stated.

Liquid and Volume Measures

Metric	Imperial	American
5 ml	$1/6$ fl oz	1 teaspoon
10 ml	$1/3$ fl oz	1 dessertspoon
15 ml	$1/2$ fl oz	1 tablespoon
60 ml	2 fl oz	$1/4$ cup (4 tablespoons)
85 ml	$2^{1}/2$ fl oz	$1/3$ cup
90 ml	3 fl oz	$3/8$ cup (6 tablespoons)
125 ml	4 fl oz	$1/2$ cup
180 ml	6 fl oz	$3/4$ cup
250 ml	8 fl oz	1 cup
300 ml	10 fl oz ($1/2$ pint)	$1^{1}/4$ cups
375 ml	12 fl oz	$1^{1}/2$ cups
435 ml	14 fl oz	$1^{3}/4$ cups
500 ml	16 fl oz	2 cups
625 ml	20 fl oz (1 pint)	$2^{1}/2$ cups
750 ml	24 fl oz	3 cups
1 litre	32 fl oz	4 cups
1.25 litres	40 fl oz (2 pints)	5 cups
1.5 litres	48 fl oz	6 cups
2.5 litres	80 fl oz (4 pints)	10 cups

Dry Measures

Metric	Imperial
30 grams	1 ounce
45 grams	$1^{1}/2$ ounces
55 grams	2 ounces
70 grams	$2^{1}/2$ ounces
85 grams	3 ounces
100 grams	$3^{1}/2$ ounces
110 grams	4 ounces
125 grams	$4^{1}/2$ ounces
140 grams	5 ounces
280 grams	10 ounces
450 grams	16 ounces, 1 pound
500 grams	1 pound, $1^{1}/2$ ounces
700 grams	$1^{1}/2$ pounds
800 grams	$1^{3}/4$ pounds
1 kilogram	2 pounds, 3 ounces
1.5 kilograms	3 pounds, $4^{1}/2$ ounces
2 kilograms	4 pounds, 6 ounces

Oven Temperature

	°C	°F	Gas Regulo
Very slow	120	250	1
Slow	150	300	2
Moderately slow	160	325	3
Moderate	180	350	4
Moderately hot	190/200	375/400	5/6
Hot	210/220	410/425	6/7
Very hot	230	450	8
Super hot	250/290	475/550	9/10

Length

Metric	Imperial
0.5 cm	$1/4$ inch
1 cm	$1/2$ inch
1.5 cm	$3/4$ inch
2.5 cm	1 inch

"Food takes us back to another place and time. The aroma of freshly baked bread, the cracking of roasted pig skin and even the way a dish is presented— these bring to mind certain times in our lives. And even if we forget them, a simple whiff or a subtle taste can easily transport us back to those moments."

Acknowledgements

Your undeniable talent and hard work clearly show on these pages, but what may not be evident on print are your loyalty, support and generosity that have consequently made this a project that's beyond me. No words can ever say how much I am thankful to have worked with each one of you. My heartfelt gratitude.

At Maculangan whose flair for photography and creativity continue to surprise and inspire me. I can always trust you to bring out the best in my work.

Aileen Anastacio who shoves me when all I needed was a push. Your ideas and words of comfort never fail to put me back on track.

To Lydia Leong and her team for keeping up with my level of intensity. Thanks for acknowledging and fuelling my passion.

To the contributors who shared their treasured recipes and let us into an intimate part of their lives. Your spirit of giving drives me to do more than what I am capable of doing.

And of course, to our Almighty God, for continually guiding me throughout this wonderful journey.

The Author

Ever since his foray into food five years ago, Angelo Comsti has had his finger in too many pies. Still, he manages to do all of them pretty well. He is a food writer, having written for television and various periodicals, both print and digital; and a food and prop stylist, having produced delicious works for magazines, TV and print ads, billboards, restaurant menus and bestselling cookbooks. On occasion, he develops recipes for corporate clients and food magazines as well as holds cooking demonstrations. He also has a regular FM radio spot called Radio Brunch on Manila's Wave 89.1 where he talks about all things food.

Angelo finished professional culinary studies at Le Cordon Bleu in Sydney, Australia. He co-authored Home-made for the Holidays and lives in Manila, Philippines.

Thank you for allowing us to share the food and memories that have made our lives delicious. Here's to family feasts— from our table to yours!

Angelo